I0521633

SEX EDUCATION
FOR TEENS

Understanding Sex, Sexuality, and Relationships. The Things Teens Don't Want to Ask Their Parents

KATHY WYNNE

FOREWORD

I am honoured to have been invited to read SEX ED-
UCATION FOR TEENS by Kathy Wynne. I found
reading this book approachable for all ages. The topics are relevant to today's teenagers and adults who
may want to understand the sensitive and essential issues of sexual health. I enjoy the positive outlook on
the elements surrounding relationships and how there
are good questions to help foster discussions. As a
school counselor, and in my study of SEXUAL
HEALTH EDUCATION IN THE CLASSROOM,
I find when adults have a source that helps generate a
positive outlook on the elements of sexual health,
their confidence in having conversations with teenagers increases. Subsequently develops a healthy relationship with teenagers who are curious about sexual
health. This book provides an understanding that en-
courages positive curiosity so that the reader is sup-
plied with accurate present-day information so anyone can have a healthy conversation with other adults

or professionals. The questions and examples in each chapter allow the individual reader to develop their own set of values and seek out appropriate support when needed. I enjoyed the positive tone and style on the significant topic of sexual health.

Lisa Perizzolo

Lisa Perizzolo, MEd. SHEC

TABLE OF CONTENTS

Introduction.. 1

Chapter 1: You Like Who You Like 9

Crushes.. 15

Sexual Attraction and Orientation 16

Labels 18

Sexual Orientation... 22

Gender Identity 24

Gender Expression.. 25

Finding Help and Support with Your Sexuality 26

Chapter 2: Is It Time to Start Dating? 27

Understanding What "Dating" is All About 28

The Upside of Dating? 30

Self-Discovery 31

Communication and Intimacy 31

Thoughtfulness and Caring.............................. 32

Independence 32

Are You Ready to Date?...................................... 33

How to Tell When Someone Likes You............. 36

How to Ask Someone Out.................................. 39

Dating Basics... 42

Tips for Teen Dating.. 46

Tip #1: Date Someone You're Comfortable Spending Time With 46

Tips #2: Don't Forget to Learn 47

Tip #3: Clarify Your Purpose with Your Date 47

Tip #4: Remember that Love Isn't Just an Emotion 48

Tip #5: Know the Difference Between Bad and Good Conflict...48

Tip #6: Never Ignore Red Flags 49

Tip #7: Know When to Call It Quits 49

Tip #8: Be Responsible and Safe....................50

Tip #9: Move On 50

Tip #10: Don't Rush 51

Hookups and Sexual Encounters....................51

Chapter 3: It's Getting Serious........................54

Appropriate Relationships 60

What Are Healthy Relationships are Like?.........61

Unhealthy Relationships 65

Some Signs of an Abusive Relationship..............67

How to Cope an Unhealthy Relationship..........68

Dos and Don'ts in Relationships 70

Don't Stay Away From Friends........................71

Do Be Your Own Person.................................71

Don't Hide From Issues 71

Identifying Good Against Bad Conflicts............ 72

Handling Conflicts and Difficulties in
Relationships 72

What to do During a Conflict 73

Cheating... 75

Breaking Up and Move On 76

Breaking Up With Someone 77

Moving On From a Relationship 78

Chapter 4: Let's Talk About Sex 81

Limitations of Sex Education in Schools............ 82

Why Do You Need to Learn About Sex? 84

Why Do People Have Sex? 86

Should You Have Sex?... 89

Why Wait? 91

When Are You Ready for Sex?............................ 92

Wrong Reasons to Have Sex 95

How Teens Can Resist Sexual Pressure............ 101

Chapter 5: Yes, You May Not! 103

Consent.. 106

Getting Consent 107

How to Ask for Consent..................................... 109

Signs of Consent... 111

Signs of Non-Consent..................................... 111

How to Establish Boundaries............................ 112

Sexual Assault and Violence 113

Handling Sexual Harassment 115

Sexual Violence 117

Protecting Yourself 119

What to Do if You Become a Victim 120

Chapter 6: Accidents Happen 122

Pregnancy...123

Sexually Transmitted Diseases (STDs) 126

Protecting Yourself 127

    Birth Control or Contraception 135
    Birth Control Pills, Patches, and Rings 138

Less Effective Birth Control 141

Protection from STIs or STDs 143

Emergency Contraception (EC) 145

What if You or Your Partner Gets Pregnant? ...147

    What Are Your Options? 148
    Abortion...149
    Adoption..151
    Parenting 153

Misconceptions about Sex...................................156

    Myth #1: Everybody is doing it. 156
    Myth #2: Pulling out can't make her pregnant.
   157

Myth #3: Girls cannot get pregnant if they have sex during their period................................... 157

Myth #4: Real-life sex is merely like what you see in porn.. 158

Myth #5: Birth control is the girl's responsibility. 158

Myth #6: A girl does not get pregnant when having sex for the first time. 159

Chapter 7: What Happens Online 160

Online Dating.. 162

Online Predators... 165

Sexting and Sending Sensitive Photos Online.. 167

Cyberbullying.. 168

Pornography 171

Understanding Porn Addiction.................... 173

Chapter 8: Q & A 175

Conclusion.. 188

References 193

INTRODUCTION

- Are you worried about dealing with sex and relationship?

- Do you feel out of place when your peers talk about their romantic relationships?

- Do you feel the need for sex education because you can't discuss it with anyone?

- Do you want to know everything about sex but are afraid to ask?

As soon as you reach the adolescent stage, you become aware and curious about sex and relationships. You expect your relationships to provide you with social status, intimacy, and social pleasure, and you want these goals fulfilled through sex, which is quite alarming.

Today, Sexually Transmitted Diseases (STDs) are at an all-time high. Though adolescents are only a quarter of the sexually active population, the survey revealed that their ratio to those with STDs is 1:2. Young people, who are 15-24 account for half of the 26 million STD-infected population in the United States. It is pretty alarming, but how do you avoid these risks (Center for Disease Control and Prevention, 2021)?

Other concerns may include the fact that teens subjected to sexual crimes and other sexual issues were extremely confused, disgusted, and hateful of themselves, and adequate sex education could have prevented all these. In other words, you could have known what to do and where to ask for help in a situation like that.

* * * * *

"Sex is perfectly natural. It's something that's pleasurable. It's enjoyable, and it enhances a relationship. So why don't we learn as much as we can about it and become comfortable with ourselves as sexual human beings because we are all sexual?"
Sue Johanson

* * * * *

Introduction

Claire is a seventeen-year-old teenage girl who grew up in a traditional family. Because her parents worked, she was always on her own when at home. Claire would avoid hanging out with other teens in school most of the time, afraid that she had nothing to contribute to the group. She always heard the girls talking about sex, and she felt ignorant and inexperienced compared to her peers.

Like other kids in school, she was curious about sex and relationships. She also wanted to explore and experience having a boyfriend but was afraid she would make the wrong decisions about sex. Most girls in schools have been in and out of relationships. Without this experience to boast, they are questioning her sexuality. It bothers Claire as she doesn't want to be a laughingstock. But she was also worried about getting pregnant or being infected with STDs once she begins going out with boys. Claire wanted to share this matter with her mom but was too shy to bring it up. Even sex education in school isn't enough to sustain her increasing curiosity.

It may be too early for Claire's concerns about Sexually Transmitted Diseases (STDs), and only a small percent of our teen population is thinking about this possibility. But do you know that you can have STDs even without vaginal intercourse and even when you have only one partner? Another alarming fact is the statistics revealing that young people—including teens make up only 27% of the sexually-active population but account for 50% of Sexually Transmitted Infections (STIs) (American Psychological Association, 2017).

There is a lack of education about sex for this age group. If you don't want to be part of this statistic, you must get accurate information about sex and relationships even before you start having them.

Many of you could be like Claire, curious about sex and relationships, but have no one to ask – no one to give answers to those curious questions that bug most teenagers. Whatever stage you are in your life as a teen, the subject of sex education will always arouse your curiosity. You may or may not have any romantic or sexual experience, or you may be navigating through your first relationship or infatuation, but information about sex is vital to every growing kid.

However, teens' sex education does not only concern you. Even your parents are aware of what you're going through. Your parents are likewise challenged by these issues on sex and relationship, for they have been there before. It's not easy for parents to discuss this matter with their kids, although they desire to teach their teens about sex and relationships, they often don't know where to start.

Claire is just one of the many teenagers struggling because of these issues. Parents and teens alike struggle to cope with the lack of sex education, resulting in related social problems such as unwanted pregnancy, STDs, sexual harassment and violence, contraception, homosexuality, and many more.

You may have sex education in your school, but it won't suffice for the curiosity growing in you. And suppose you're one of those unfortunate kids studying in schools with no sex education in their curriculum. In that case, you will turn to social media and the internet to ebb your growing curiosity. Without someone to guide you in your choice of information, you will most likely end up viewing pornography sites, which can have detrimental consequences for years to come.

According to a research study conducted by researchers of the University of Washington, teens who receive intensive sex education are less likely to become pregnant than those with no formal sex education or taught to believe there must be no sex before marriage (Health Behavior News Service, 2008).

In countries with very traditional cultures, talking about sex is taboo. So even when there is a complete curriculum about sex education, teachers are not comfortable discussing it with teens. They feel that only those who are married should discuss such matters. It is also why many parents, even in Western culture, find it unnecessary, if not uncomfortable, to talk about sex education with their teens.

Alex McKay, Executive Director at the Sex Information and Education Council of Canada (SIECAN), divulged in research that when teenagers miss out on sex education, they are subjected to a higher risk for sexually transmitted diseases and infections with the possibility of early pregnancy. What kids learn about sexual health has a significant impact on their views of sex and behavior.

I wrote this book to address challenging issues which are troubling teens. Having children of my own -- two daughters, who are young adults, and two young boys, who will be in their teens soon, I feel I must educate others on such important issues.

Introduction

My great desire is to help all of you achieve a realistic understanding of sex and relationships while helping my own kids avoid the same problems. Hopefully, equipping you with the knowledge will encourage you to become more responsible and loving adults.

Writing this book matters greatly to me because I want to help you avoid the confusion and self-doubt that I had when I was your age. I know how capable you are of having loving and responsible relationships, even at a very young age. However, it is essential not to have a mistaken view of what is involved with sex and relationships. It is only through guiding you in the right direction that you will achieve a healthy foundation for adulthood.

As a mom with an adequate background in education, I am writing based on experience, research, and communicating with children, other teens, and parents who have shared stories about their teens in my current profession. Because I have first-hand experience raising teenagers going through the ups and downs of teen relationships, I want to help you navigate sex and relationships to avoid serious issues that could severely damage your future.

Reading this book will gain you a myriad of benefits. It is not another boring textbook of facts but a helpful guide that will present various situations you will be encountering as you grow to prepare yourself for navigating through the different stages of life.

Let's see a fraction of what you will learn.

- Detailed information that addresses the usual questions teens ask about sex and relationships.
- Learn how to navigate your first relationship.
- Know when to give your consent and how to establish and keep boundaries.
- Dating tips and how to stay safe in sex.
- Know your options in case of pregnancy.
- How to cope with heartbreaks.

Now that you know how important sex education is in shaping your future, start equipping yourself with this guide to prepare for a better life.

CHAPTER 1

YOU LIKE WHO YOU LIKE

- Is there someone whom you have a crush on in school?
- Is there a specific type of personality that attracts you?
- Do you tend to like girls, boys, or both.?

It is not surprising to feel attracted to someone. This kind of emotion is somehow more vital during the adolescence stage. You will often mistake attraction and infatuation for love. It is only later that you will realize that what you thought was love was mere attraction.

All of you may have experienced this feeling of attraction, and so we will focus this chapter on the different factors that cause your interest in another individual. Falling in love and being in a romantic relationship is part of many adolescents' timetables.

The adolescent stage can be very challenging. When hormonal changes occur, they cause you emotional disturbances, which can be very hard to manage by yourself. You can tell that you're in this stage when you feel you're not okay in all aspects of your life. You get easily irritated when corrected and yet feel helpless and remorse for your behavior at the same time.

This stage in your life can be complicated while undergoing rapid changes in your body and experiencing emotional ups and downs. Your physical body and brain are maturing fast, and you are experiencing bodily changes you have never experienced before. Because your need for attention and recognition in the adult world gets more intense, you tend to assert yourself. Peer relationships become more significant for you as the desire to explore and experiment more starts to set in. This is because the teenage years are when you begin to discover sexuality.

Sexuality includes feelings and attractions at all levels—not just to whom you have sexual encounters. While this is common in your teenage years, it can be confusing for most young people; especially those teens raised in traditional families with overprotective parents.

Working out your identity and finding where you fit in can be challenging, leading to distress, anxiety, and isolation. So, in this chapter, I will guide you through discovering your sexuality.

Having a crush or infatuation, idolizing a pop star, or getting into a relationship are just some of the influencing factors in your life. Psychologists classify these influencing factors into two categories: **situational** and **individual** characteristics.

Situational factors include familiarity, closeness, and anxiety.

Familiarity. Once you become familiar with someone, you tend to develop attraction because of constant exposure.

Closeness or proximity. Do you know why best friends often end up in a romantic relationship? Most of the time, being in each other's company develops attraction, leading to a romantic relationship.

Anxiety or Stress. Individuals with high levels of stress or anxiety tend to isolate themselves, while those with low pressure and stress are more sociable. It shows that you can develop attraction toward people you are close to, familiar with, and have a low-stress level.

Other factors are **individual factors** such as personal qualities, physical attractiveness, reciprocity of liking, and the similarity in attitude and characteristics (Rohatgi, 2015).

Personal Qualities. Individuals possessing both positive and negative qualities are more attractive than those who seem perfect. Did you notice that most girls are more attracted to bad boys than the boy-next-door type? Those who aren't flawless are also said to be more attractive than those who are flawless.

Physical Attractiveness. You are attracted to those you see as attractive in the physical sense. It sounds shallow to say that most teenagers are strongly influenced by physical attractiveness. However, popular culture prefers physical beauty.

Reciprocity of Liking. It is but natural that we like back people who want us. Even the Law of Attraction conveys this principle.

All these prove that you feel the attraction because of personal qualities, similarities in attitudes, reciprocity of liking, and when you find the other person physically attractive.

The Similarity in Attitude and Characteristics. It is normal to attract people who share similarities in attitude and characteristics. You tend to like those who are similar to you in many ways. For example, adventurous teens flock together, and so do introverts.

Regardless of age, feeling in love can be a difficult stage for you, and this even doubles when you find it hard to manage your emotions. At this point, you are maturing physically and mentally at a rate not experienced since childhood.

Aside from changes in your physical appearance, you are likewise developing secondary sex characteristics. This spurt in growth sometimes results in physical awkwardness. You feel embarrassed and self-conscious of any changes in your body, especially when they don't conform to your body ideals and when you find them inadequate.

When you are in your twenties, you become more adventurous. However, you usually have poor judgment and bad choices, especially temptations. It is because that area in your brain, the prefrontal cortex, responsible for executive functioning, develops last (Petanjek et al., 2011).

Because there is a surge in your hormonal production, you are experiencing intense sexual attraction, which is why attraction is at its height. Many of you feel strong sexual urges, risk-taking, and experience mood swings because of these hormones. It is also when you can confuse lust for love as emotions are overwhelming (Rohatgi, 2015).

It's not only sex hormones at work when you start to fall in love. There is an increase in your stress hormones – and you feel all the signs and emotions associated with being in love, rapid heart and pulse beats, sweating, and dry mouth when you see the person that attracts you. And because dopamine stimulates your desire and pleasure, which is like the feeling of being high — this effect is also experienced when taking drugs. It takes time to fall in love.

However, it is through these romantic relationships that you can grow psychologically. You learn more about yourself and other people. When in a romantic relationship, you gain experiences like managing your emotions, developing intimacy skills, and facing new risks and challenges in life (The British Psychological Society, 2016).

Crushes

You will experience crushes before you finally get into a steady relationship. **Identity crush** happens when you idolize someone you want to be identified with, as in pop idols or famous students on their campus, like a varsity player or head of the group.

On the other hand, a **romantic crush** starts when you feel romantic about another person. You imagine that person as someone ideal or perfect. Romantic crushes often don't last long and quickly vanish once you know them. Because teens' feelings are intense, you are greatly affected when others make fun of your romantic interest in another.

Sexual development in young people includes experience and relationships - even same-sex attraction, which is why other teens develop a bisexual interest

(Raising Children Network (Australia) Limited, n.d.).

Usually, pre-teens and teenagers are pretty clear about their preferences - e.g., you are clear about your feelings and what attracts you. However, don't feel discouraged if you realize that you're different from others or what the media presents.

Sexual Attraction and Orientation

At some stage, it is normal for most of you to experiment with some aspects of sex like:

- ♦ Sexual attraction
- ♦ Sexual behavior
- ♦ Sexual identity
- ♦ Gender identity

Being curious about sex is a natural and intense urge during these years. However, not all teenage relationships result in sex.

As you grow mature in years, you are likewise maturing emotionally and socially. You might want a more intimate romantic relationship to express your love and affection to your partner. You may also be curious and want to explore adult behavior at some point.

According to new research, teens have a sexual orientation even when not sexually active (Canadian Paediatric Society, 2018). Here are how people are classified based on sexual orientation.

- **Heterosexuals** are those attracted to people of the opposite sex. They are also what we call straight.

- **Lesbians** are women attracted to the same sex. On the other side, gays are those men who are attracted to other men. **Gay** is sometimes also used to describe lesbians as well.

- **Bisexuals** are those who are attracted to two or more sexes.

- **Pansexual** is a kind of attraction based on sex, gender, or gender identity.

- **Demisexuals** are those who have no sexual attraction without a strong emotional connection.

♦ **Asexuals** are those who lack any sexual attraction.

Teens have different sexual orientations. Sexual orientation is the emotional, romantic, or sexual attraction a person feels toward another person. You may be sexually attracted to either someone of the opposite sex or someone of the same sex as you. Some even become bisexual, while others may have no desire for sex (Raising Children Network, 2021).

Labels

As we have mentioned before, it is normal for you to explore and experiment with your sexuality during the development process. Later you will realize that your sexuality changes over time. According to research conducted by Carolina State University and the University of Pittsburgh, at least one in every five teenagers reported some changes in sexual orientation (Shipman, 2019).

Coming Out

While you are still in your adolescent stage, you can't label yourself as gay, straight, or anything else.

However, there are many reasons you may choose to come out. Here are some of the reasons.

- ◆ You are ready to go out dating and want your family and close friends to know.

- ◆ You don't want other people making assumptions and gossiping about you.

- ◆ You are tired of hearing other people use stereotypes or label you negatively.

- ◆ You feel like you are living a lie or not being honest with yourself. You want other people to accept you for who you are.

On the other hand, there are also many reasons for you to hide in your closet (Raising Children Network (Australia) Limited, n.d.).

- ◆ You are not sure of your sexuality or how you feel. You are still trying to figure out who you are.

- ◆ You consider sexual orientation or gender private and see no reason to discuss it with other people.

- ◆ You are afraid that others will bully, harass, discriminate against, or abuse you once you choose to come out.

- ◆ Your families are not aware of your sexuality, and you worry that your parents and siblings can't accept you.

Remember that your sexuality is a matter of personal choice, and only you can make this decision.

So when you decide to come out in the open, you have to keep these in mind.

Trust your gut. Trust your gut, and don't feel forced or threatened. When you have discovered something about yourself you may want to share it with friends and family, or you may want to keep it to yourself.

It is natural to hesitate to come out and declare that you are a member of the LGBTQ community. You may wonder what to do once you share this with your family and friends. It sure will turn your world upside down. If you choose to share this with just a few friends, can you trust them not to broadcast it?

The decision to come out can be more complicated if you still depend on your parents. Depending on your culture, you will find it easier to gain support from family. However, each of you has different things that you need to consider. Most of you come out gradually by telling a few friends at the start of seeking the help of a therapist. Some call an LGBTQ support group to help them emotionally regarding their identity or coming out.

Weigh all the possibilities before making your final decision. You have to ask yourself first before deciding to come out.

- Is it worth it?
- Will it not be easy for me to come out?
- How could I make things easier?

Weigh the outcome of every possibility based on what you expect their reactions will be.

Have a Support System. If you are still hesitant to come out openly, afraid that your parents can't accept you for what you are, speak to a counselor or contact an anonymous helpline such as the LGBTQ National Youth Talkline.

With a support system in place, you can choose whether to come out in the open or keep this decision to yourself. Support systems can help you cope with your emotions if reactions to your coming out are not acceptable to people around you or if you need an emergency shelter.

Think about privacy. You may know some people—a friend or a relative who are mature enough to respect you for what you are and keep whatever private information you have shared with them. However, for every piece of information you relay to someone, it is always possible to leak out.

Sexual Orientation

Sexual orientation is the sexual attraction and feelings of romance one individual has for another. It is a matter of who you are drawn to and want to be in a relationship with. It may be your attraction to the opposite sex (heterosexuality), same-sex (homosexuality), to both sex (bisexuality), all genders (pansexual), or neither (asexuality).

Sexual orientation is different from gender identity. Gender identity is not about attractions but about who you are as a person - are you male, female, queer, etc.?

It means that being transgender isn't the same as being gay, lesbian, or bisexual. Sexual orientation is about who you want, while gender identity is about who you are.

Gender identity is quite a complicated issue for teens. Some people don't think that any of these labels describe them accurately. There are even those who don't want to be labeled at all. While others are comfortable being labeled, others aren't, and whether or not you label your self is solely your choice.

Although not all are comfortable accepting the idea of sexual orientation, differences and prejudices still exist, and homosexuality is no longer a big deal in today's society. However, even when LGBTQ members gain more acceptance and become more visible in our society, there are still people who don't agree with them.

For those who aren't straight, fears of prejudice, rejection, and bullying lead them to keep their sexual orientation to themselves, aware that their family and friends will not support them. This fear leads LGBTQ teens to have higher rates of homelessness, self-harm, mental health conditions, and suicide. Those openly accepted and supported by friends and families live happier and healthier lives as adults.

Gender Identity

Gender Identity is how you describe yourself. Each individual's experience with their gender identity is unique and personal.

Some people think that only two gender identities are possible: boy or girl. Many people experience having a gender outside of these two primary selections. Some identify themselves with both genders (as both a boy and a girl.) Others are neither. There are also others identifying their gender other than a boy or girl. Others don't experience gender at all. Those who don't share a whole gender, either male or female, have non-binary genders and there are many ways to be non-binary.

Throughout history and worldwide, people are experiencing diverse genders. While they are identified with the sex they are born with, some find their identity gender different from their assigned sex at birth. Exploring your gender is expected at all ages and at any stage of life. All of these experiences are equally valid. It helps to imagine how you experience gender.

Gender Expression

Gender Expression describes how you present yourself, including how you look, dress, style your hair, and behave.

Gender identity is different from gender expression. It is essential not to assume that the way someone moves, talks, dresses, or styles their hair indicates how they identify their gender. There are many fantastic ways to be a person of a different gender. Boys have opted to wear dresses, girls have short hair, and some non-binary folks wear makeup.

Gender expression is all about how you want to present yourself to others. Even if you can't express your gender the way you want it, it is still you!

How would you like to present your gender? How do you want to express it? What aspect of gender expression can make you happy and feel like you are genuine and not a fake?

Finding Help and Support with Your Sexuality

Many can't openly talk about their sexual orientation because others belong to a family or community where gays are not accepted or respected. Because they are not accepted by other people, including their family, friends, and culture, they can't openly talk about their sexual orientation.

It can help teens talk to someone about the confusing feeling of growing up–whether that person is your parent, friend, sibling, or counselor. There are communities or youth groups that can give LGBTQ teens the chance to communicate with other teens, who are in the same situations. Psychologists, psychiatrists, doctors, and trained counselors can help you cope with the problems of developing sexuality–in private and with confidentiality.

Regardless of what you like, your teen years are the right time to explore and learn more about yourself and your preferences–a part of which is dating and hanging out with teen friends or the people of your interest.

CHAPTER 2

IS IT TIME TO START DATING?

As a teen, this is the time you tend to be curious about romantic relationships. And believe me, this is all perfectly natural. Your parents, grandparents, and the adults around you have gone through this stage.

Having a crush or being sexually attracted to someone doesn't make you anything other than human. You need not feel guilty when you develop a romantic interest in a classmate sitting next to you or the doe-eyed cheerleader with a cute dimple. Yes, you may feel embarrassed or awkward about your feelings toward that person, but that doesn't signify that you've made a mistake.

When a person becomes fascinated by someone or something on a romantic level, their curiosity leads to a certain point where they want to learn more about the object of their interest. When the object of curiosity reciprocates this feeling, spending time with each other serves as the stepping stone toward a much deeper bond. This getting-to-know process is known to us as "dating."

Understanding What "Dating" is All About

Many parents easily freak out when their young adolescent kids ask, "Mom/Dad, would it be okay to go out on a date?" It might sound super simple since you're only asking a question answerable with a plain yes or no. However, this seemingly simple inquiry links to a series of topics they need to discuss with you, issues that many adults find extremely challenging to raise.

So, before we can take this subject further, I would like you to ponder on these:

♦ What is dating all about for you?

- ♦ What do you think happens during a date?
- ♦ What is your idea of a "perfect" date?

Building social bonds at this stage is part of your exploration of life and what goes on in it. You begin experimenting with its many aspects to help you determine what suits your personality and style. Of course, this is very much true in building relationships regardless of their nature.

Adolescents like you typically socialize in mixed-gender groups within or outside school. Group activities like going to the movies, attending parties, or playing volleyball at the beach can allow teenagers to mingle easily in the dating pool. You can easily get caught up with how fast things happen. Therefore, it is be best for you to be mentally prepared by reflecting on how to answer the questions such as listed above.

How you perceive "dating" is a crucial aspect of this discussion because your perspective can dictate your behavior during this process. For example, younger adolescents may view dating as an activity involving hanging out with a special someone and sharing the problems they encounter growing up. Meanwhile, older adolescents have more complex ideas about dating, especially nowadays. They tend to categorize dating as being "casual," wherein both parties are not yet ready for a steady commitment, and you're just enjoying each other's company. Some want to have an "open" dating relationship, which is the opposite of "exclusive" dating. Others express their intent to date thoughtfully, which means they're ready for a serious commitment.

You see, dating isn't limited to watching movies, going out to eat, or going to an amusement park with the person you like. These are only some highlights of your entire dating experience. There's much more in between these romantic activities. It may start as simply as those, but eventually, they evolve.

The Upside of Dating?

Dating is an excellent method to bond with your special person. It's an enjoyable way to explore your feelings and get to know the other person. While all of these are true, you might have overlooked some advantages you gain from dating.

Romantic relationships enable teens like you to improve their confidence, sense of identity, interpersonal skills, emotion, empathy, and intimacy. Life experiences revolving around this type of relationship offer invaluable fundamentals for long-term relation-ships in the future. They are powerful contributors to many facets of your adolescent life, including but not limited to your growth, happiness, and resilience.

Self-Discovery

Your teen years are considered the formative stage of your life, and dating allows you to see who you are as a person. You learn about your limitations and boundaries, such as:

- Recognizing the things you like, prefer, and dislike
- Defining which actions are acceptable or not to be tolerated
- When to pursue and when to stop

Eventually, these factors will be the basis of your choices and goals in future relationships.

Communication and Intimacy

Teen dating can be harnessed as a tool to hone your communication skills. Take this opportunity to improve your ability to listen, negotiate, and compro-mise. Remember that healthy communication skills involve honesty, respect, and being open about your feelings. Moreover, you learn that relationships that value trust, closeness, and support significantly contribute to a positive outlook in life.

Thoughtfulness and Caring

Teenagers who date become developed in the realms of caring and thoughtfulness. One of the reasons might be that they tend to be more sensitive to the needs of the person they're in a relationship with. They practice recognizing subtle hints in the other person's behavior that conveys pleasure, dislike, anger, fatigue, and other hidden emotions. We tend to overlook these minor aspects in a relationship with our friends and family but become more sensitive when our romantic partner is involved.

Independence

According to a study, quality dating relationships during adolescent years play a part in your future well-being, including your sense of identity and autonomy. Conversely, having toxic romantic relationships may cause you to engage in unhealthy romantic patterns that will ultimately be detrimental to your psychosocial functioning (Kansky & Allen, 2018).

Are You Ready to Date?

Peer pressure is a powerful force on how teenagers decide on something, which is natural since everybody wants to be "in," or at least average. Anyone can relate to this when it comes to dating. You may have seen your friends dating, so you consider dating, too. However, this shouldn't be the case because how you date during your adolescence is a strong predictor of how you can handle relationships during your adulthood.

If you're not ready to date yet and merely joined the dating fad because your friends are doing it, there is a greater chance that you will develop negative relationship behaviors. You might also hurt the person you date because your feelings and views about dating or relationships do not align.

Everyone is different, and your decision on when to start dating should not depend on what's currently popular. So, don't mind when your peers tell you to date this guy or girl because you "seem" good for each other or you must start dating because they're already doing it. Bear in mind that relationships involve authentic choice, not dependency.

You can tell that you're ready to date when:

You have a stable sense of worth. Do you see yourself as someone confident in or out of a relationship? Or do you see yourself struggling with your own identity? Perhaps, you still need more time to know who you are before trying to be with someone. You don't need to "know yourself perfectly," but just enough to clearly define who you are at present, what you like and dislike, and what you believe you deserve as a human being.

You are open to learning how to communicate. Communication is imperative in any relationship, and it's a good thing that it can be learned. Practice with your existing relationships, such as with family and friends. For instance, calmly communicate with your parents even if you're upset or frustrated instead of choosing to shout or walk away from them.

You are willing to learn about compromise. Your ability to compromise significantly impacts the quality of any of your relationships. Like communication, compromising needs to be practiced. For example, you and a friend want to hang out but have different ideas about what to do. Let's say that you want to go to the park, but they want to go to the bookstore. You can try to compromise by saying you can visit the bookstore first before heading to the park.

You genuinely like someone. Like I said before, you don't have to date just for the sake of dating. That would eventually create conflict between yourself and the other party involved. Instead, date when there is someone you would like to get to know and spend time with.

You know what healthy relationships look like. Teen dating should inspire you, not stress you out.

Your parents gave you their signal. Of course, your parent's opinion matters because of two main reasons. Firstly, they are your PARENTS who take care, guide, and protect you. And secondly, you might still be underage and need proper guidance, which leads you back to the first reason.

Being in a relationship doesn't necessarily mean that it's the right thing for you. You are still very young and can afford to take things slowly. You can still be cool and single while taking the time to get to know more about yourself. There is no need to require yourself to do what everybody else is doing because you want to be cool and popular.

How to Tell When Someone Likes You

It could be one of the toughest questions you will ever have to answer in your youth. Everybody who has liked someone in their teens asked it at least once. Even adults, — in their 20s, 30s, 40s — and even beyond — who have crushes come across this pondering.

You might encounter different scenarios that may lead you to ask if someone likes you. Here are some of them:

If they're sending vague signals that they're crushing on you. Have you ever caught someone looking at you from afar, smiling at you every time you meet in the corridors, or looking away bashfully whenever your eyes meet? It may leave you thinking they like you, but you cannot be sure about it. You don't want to base your conclusion on these seemingly ambiguous variables.

If they're flirting with you. You may have met this type— someone who is stylish, friendly, popular, and knows exactly what to say every time. Sometimes, someone's warm smile can make you feel so special. Or actions of another person can pique your interest and confuse you simultaneously.

Suppose they're more than just a friend, but not a lover. Perhaps, you have someone who's glued by your side, cuddles with you, and gets jealous when you're admiring a hot classmate. Other people even think of you as a couple, but this person quickly corrects them that you're not.

Being in one of these situations will only leave you exhausted over time. Therefore, it's crucial to determine whether the other person, especially if you're also interested in them, likes you or not. Let these questions guide you to the answer you're looking for:

Do they shower you with a lot of attention? Maybe they exert more effort to be with you? For example, they always grab a seat with you during lunch, or they wait for you so that you can go home together.

Do they focus their attention on you even when with other people? Perhaps they go straight to you and talk with you even if you're with a group of friends. Or maybe they find every opportunity to speak with you and even stay longer than needed.

Do they maintain eye contact with you? Holding your gaze can indicate that they like you, as such is the case for confident individuals. On the other hand, the shy ones tend to quickly get embarrassed whenever you try to establish eye contact with them.

Do they often share personal matters only with you? What do they usually talk to you about? Do they share their dreams or plans after graduation? How about emotional problems? Do they ask about your goals during summer vacation, hinting they want to spend some time with you?

More positive answers to these questions mean a greater chance that the other person likes you. If you're still doubtful, assessing the situation with your best friends can help. However, if you're the bold and straightforward type, it would be best to ask the person directly.

How to Ask Someone Out

"Who is supposed to ask out first?" you may ask. Girls, especially those from conservative families, tend to shy away from confessing their feelings to the person they like. Most people from older generations tend to say that females should be the ones admitted to and not the ones to confess — that boys should take the initiative.

This old-fashioned belief doesn't make any sense for a girl who aims to catch the interest of the boy she likes. Wouldn't it be less complicated if you, who want the other person, confessed your feelings? What if you're a girl who likes another girl? How would this rule suit your situation? Hence, the boy-asks-girl rule is now considered outdated.

Feel free to express your feelings regardless of your gender role. Common sense dictates that the person who likes another should be the one to reach out. It doesn't necessarily mean that you should ask the other person to date them instantly, but to simply:

- ◆ Express your interest
- ◆ Determine if the other party is also interested in you

♦ Suggest that you spend time getting to know each other better

If they clearly expressed that they're also interested in you, you're ready for the next step.

Now that the "who's-going-to-ask-first" issue has been clarified let us address our main concern. How do you ask someone to go on a date?

Before anything else, get to know them a little. Find out their interests, dislikes, and hobbies. Through your interaction pay attention to their responses. Be attentive and take an active role in listening. Over the course of your conversations you'll pick up some useful information about them.

Test the waters. Try to drop off some hints about your feelings from time to time to gauge their reaction. You can also send them love notes or invitations to accompany you for an after-school snack.

Create an action plan. Jot down your best ideas and create a blueprint on how you can execute them. Make sure to consider various factors and a plan B if all else fails. When you understand what you're doing, you increase your chances of getting their approval.

Don't use cheesy and corny pickup lines. If you don't want to turn off your date, avoid using awkward lines such as, "If I have the authority to rearrange the alphabet, I will put U and I together" or "Are you tired? You keep running through my mind!"

Be ready for rejection. As sad as it may sound, things might not go the way you would like. Maybe you're not the right person for them and vice versa. Don't take it too personally, but as part of your learning about love and life.

On the contrary, you may be the one being confessed to by another, but you're not interested in dating them or anybody else. You can refuse, of course, but make sure to reject politely. You may say, "I'm thankful for your feelings, but I don't think I'm ready to go out with anyone," or "I'm flattered, but sorry, I'm not interested." And despite being cool about their love confession, you don't have to give them an explanation why you choose not to go out with them.

Dating Basics

What do you expect to happen on a date? You might quickly reply, "Oh, I've seen a lot of those in romantic comedies I've been binging." Unfortunately, dating in real life might be far from your expectations based on the films you've watched so far.

Over the years, technology has revolutionized the dating game. With the ever-rising popularity of smartphones and social media usage, teens can easily hang out even when they're continents apart. Despite today's technological progress, some truths about teen dating stay the same. Here are some of those:

- First dates are not always romantic, sweet, and fairytale-like.
- Your date might not end in a romantic relationship.
- Dating can enhance your relationship skills.
- Dates might lead to sexual activities.
- Dating might cause depression.

Take note that dating is all about getting to know each other romantically. I'm not encouraging you to go on a date when you are still too young, especially without your parents' permission. However, you will experience dating sooner or later, and it is better to be prepared before it happens. Acknowledging these truths will enable you to date wisely. It will also help you meet the right person to date— perhaps, be your girlfriend or boyfriend.

Before attempting to go out on a date with anyone, it is important to know what kind of person you want to connect with. It is also important to create a list of qualifications you require for someone you want to connect with. Be more specific with your requirements, such as detailing what qualities you are looking for and those you consider red flags. Determining these will allow you to decide what kind of relationship you want to establish with this special someone.

Let me provide you with some ideas for your checklist:

Personal Qualities	Interests and Hobbies
Age: (same age up to 3 years older)	Mobile and video games
Petite and slender	Camping
Kind and sweet	Reading
Smart but not bookish	

Respectful and polite	I prefer someone who shares the same interest as me.
Turn-Offs	
Poor personal hygiene	Spiteful and jealous-type
Disrespectful	Invades my privacy

Once you understand what type of person better suits you, start planning your first date. It is crucial to lay out your basic plans even before asking someone out or being asked out. It would help if you were prepared ahead of time since dates involve planning and risks.

One of the most straightforward and practical methods to bring your plans to fruition is to create some casual connection with the person you're planning to date. Befriending them on social media and messaging them is a great way to test the waters. However, avoid meeting with strangers online or meeting someone you just met online.

You may befriend your "crush in school" or one in the neighborhood to know them better or to start a connection, but not a total stranger. Many teens have become a victim of abuse or abduction because they go out on a date with someone they just met online.

Go the extra mile in getting to know them by looking at their social media posts from time to time. It is surprising to know how much information you can garner about them through this simple activity. Based on their online posts, you can gauge their mood, plans for the day, personality, and outlook on life.

Another reminder that you should never forget is to consult your parents about your plans. They will always be your beacon of light to steer you as you grow. They will guide and direct you to the right path and equip you with the knowledge teens should know before delving into dating or romantic relationships.

Understand that while talking about this matter with your parents could be tricky, it is more difficult on their part to explain these things to you. So, be considerate about their feelings, too.

Don't hesitate to talk to your parents about rules and expectations. They might demand that you bring a chaperone or impose curfew hours, but that's okay. That's how they can protect you. And you, in return, should not betray their trust so that you will stay trustworthy in their eyes.

Tips for Teen Dating

Before we talk about dating per se, please understand that I am not encouraging you to go dating when you are still too young. It is essential that you have your parents' permission before going out on a date with someone.

However, it is important that you have to be prepared when the time comes and you want to go on a date with someone. Below are some insights that will boost the probability of success of your dating experience:

Tip #1: Date Someone You're Comfortable Spending Time With

You're comfortable with someone when:
- You can be yourself around them
- You don't feel pressured to do things you don't want to do
- You can have different opinions on a particular matter, but they respect your opinion nevertheless

♦ You both trust each other even when you're far apart

Tips #2: Don't Forget to Learn

Let's get real—the primary purpose of young relationships is to seek out those with whom you don't belong. This may be contrary to your feelings and perspective about romance, but the truth is that many teen dating or romantic relationships don't survive. Your only consolation for this is the knowledge you acquire through experience, and using this knowledge in the future enables you to render wise decisions.

Tip #3: Clarify Your Purpose with Your Date

Convey your dating purpose as clearly as you can. Do you want to date special friends with no commitment? Do you want it to be an open, casual, or exclusive relationship? Are you serious about your feelings for the other person? It is best to determine what the real score between you is.

Tip #4: Remember that Love Isn't Just an Emotion

I encourage you to find balance despite your feelings. It's much more than showering the other person with gifts, kisses, or romantic promises. Instead, it's about giving practical attention to detail, like uplifting the person when they feel down or studying well together so both of you pass a test.

Tip #5: Know the Difference Between Bad and Good Conflict

Conflict itself is not always a bad thing. Sometimes it can bring you and your boyfriend or girlfriend closer. These rules will show you how conflicts can help your relationship become healthier:

- Listen and try to understand how your boyfriend or girlfriend feels
- Take time to explain how you feel as well
- Never bring up past disagreements
- Do not nitpick
- Avoid generalizations and talk about something productive

Tip #6: Never Ignore Red Flags

As you get to know each other gradually, ensure that you do not overlook red flags, such as:

- Embarrassing, taunting, and making you the subject of crude jokes
- Excessive jealousy or insecurity
- Bouts of anger and rage
- Controlling or pressuring you to do something you don't want to do
- Intimidation (e.g., leering looks, painful grips, threats, or using your fear against you)
- Physical abuse (e.g., throwing objects at you, slapping, scratching, hitting, and gripping you tightly)
- Taking and sharing inappropriate pictures or videos of you

Tip #7: Know When to Call It Quits

Abusive relationships happen even in young relationships. When you have noticed a red flag, it's time to break your relationship off. Ask your friends, family, and the authorities for help should the other person become violent and threaten to hurt you. Remember, you should never subject yourself to any negative behavior from your boyfriend or girlfriend.

One red flag is all you need to put a stop to the relationship. You are worth more than that.

Tip #8: Be Responsible and Safe

Sexual activity has been a part of the normal scope of adolescent development. Therefore, you must learn to be safe and responsible before engaging in sexual activity with your special someone.

While sex is a controversial topic, it's still best to discuss it with your parents. Don't get second-hand information (or misinformation) from your fellow teens. Your parents should be your go-to people when it comes to this issue.

Tip #9: Move On

As I mentioned before, teen romance can be short-lived. Understanding this can spare you unnecessary stress, and even depression. While breakups can be painful and make you "feel like dying," it doesn't mean you won't heal over time. Besides, a split-up implies that there is someone out there meant for you, and now you're free to meet them.

Tip #10: Don't Rush

Youth is the time to learn and explore a lot of new things, so enjoy it. You don't need to commit yourself to a dating marathon merely because everybody is doing it. Dating and romance aren't everything this life has to offer.

Hookups and Sexual Encounters

You may have heard a classmate talking about how they messed around with someone during a party or a friend who openly says that a certain someone is their "sex buddy." You may also be familiar with terms such as

- ◆ Hookup or hooking up
- ◆ Flings
- ◆ Messing around
- ◆ Friends with benefits or FWB
- ◆ Hanging out

People who engage in these so-called *labels* practice sexual activities together, but this doesn't mean they are committed to each other. Their sexual practices may include kissing, petting, oral sex, and sexual intercourse. These activities are purely transactional, which means that the two parties consent to have sex.

Hookups and casual sex aren't a modern-day phenomenon but have been present for over half a century. Unfortunately, it is running more rampant partly because of the easy access to various information they acquire via the internet and what media portrays about sex. An article in the Boston Magazine May 2003 issue reports that the sexualization of teen culture over the years has contributed to the drastic change in the younger generations' dating habits. Social media and unrestricted access to online information about sex and relationships have also changed teenagers' perspectives on monogamy and marriage.

As hookups are becoming the norm, there's a danger that dating and long-term relationships will no longer focus on an average teenager's romantic life.

According to research, about 75% of teenagers have their first sexual experience while dating, and the majority of sexually active teens have experienced sexual experiences without being in a romantic relationship (Manning et al., 2005).

Despite the ever-growing popularity of hookups or casual sex, **you still have the power to decide whether to take part in this kind of sexual activity or not.**

You may say that it's your body, so it's your choice. However, know that by taking advantage of this freedom, you also become **vulnerable to the repercussions of your decisions.** There will always be the possibility of unwanted pregnancies, STDs, and even mental health risks such as depression.

Hookups or casual sex aren't for everyone. They may or may not work out for you, and that's okay! Just remember that **you always have the right to say 'no' to the things you don't want to do.**

CHAPTER 3

IT'S GETTING SERIOUS

D o you remember the song, "first love never dies..."? Few of us ever forget our first love. I had my first love in high school. He was sweet and soft only when he was alone with me. I can still remember how distressed I was when we parted ways. I thought I would never recover from it, but I did when I married and had kids.

Of course, I recovered, but that first love feeling served a significant purpose in my development.

I learned how to interact with a larger world beyond my family and form healthy relationships with other people. It helped expand my little world to accommodate people I didn't know and hadn't met before.

Romantic relationships are a major developmental milestone in your life as a teen. They come with all the other physical, emotional, and social changes in your adolescent stage.

This kind of emotion is too intense because it goes back to evolution. It is all about love and a sense of belonging, which are our deepest motivations and tied to our understanding of human survival.

Relationships for teens can be too intense because they lack the experience that creates a broader perspective of things and is highly attuned to what others think of them. For example, when a romantic partner can't reply when their interest (or boyfriend/girlfriend) text them, they are more likely to feel rejected and easily irked. They fail to think that there may be other reasons behind the other person's lack of reply. They also get easily angry because, during the teenage years, there is a lack of inhibitory abilities while their executive brain functioning is still developing. While going through the experience of romantic love, you can use this as a teaching moment.

Romantic relationships have much to teach the young generation about communication, emotions, empathy, identity, and sex in some couples. Relationships involving teens often involve exploring physical intimacy and sexual feelings and can teach you lessons for future relationships. Your first romantic relationships are an excellent opportunity to understand what it means to be in a relationship. And while these lessons can provide you with a valuable foundation for long-term relationships in adulthood, they are likewise significant contributors to growth, resilience, and happiness during your teenage years.

There is no right age to be in a relationship. However, know that changes occur between 9-19 years old. Starting from 9-11, you might be exhibiting more independence from your family. When you reach 10-15, you begin to feel attraction, and when you're 15-19, romantic relationships can be central to your life as a teen. It is also common for children not to be interested in romantic relationships until they reach their late teens. But in a study conducted by researchers from the Harvard Graduate School of Education, several teens and young adults reported not being ready for caring, lasting romantic relationships and are anxious about developing them (Action Canada for Sexual Health and Rights, 2019).

Teens learn about the various kinds of love as they go out dating. There is something pure and unique about your first love. This love may not last forever, but it's something with magical memories. Unlike adults, you may not want to believe or hear adults say that young love won't last forever.

If you are in high school or early college, you may have experienced having severe romantic relationships. If it's not traumatic, it could be a good opportunity for you to understand what it is to be in a healthy relationship. With this experience, you can continue to have a healthy relationship throughout your life.

While you are in a relationship, you must have a good relationship and communication with your parents—daughter to mom and son to dad. You may get curious about many things, but exploring them on your own can sometimes be disastrous when there's no one there to guide you. It's typical for teens to be curious about sexuality, and just like the adage, curiosity kills a cat; it could be too late when you realize it.

It's always best to feel comfortable sharing secrets with your mom or your dad, and this can only be possible if you have established a close relationship with them. What you don't know may frighten you, which is also applicable to your parents. When they are not aware of what's happening in your life, they are afraid to trust you. Parents always feel that their kids are too young to go dating or be in a relationship—considering that they have been there before you when they were your age.

Suppose you want your parents to trust you, better start on the right foot. When they can understand you, they will know why you need to go out on a date, and they can teach you the right thing to do to protect yourself. This is why it is essential to maintain your bond with your parents from childhood to adolescence.

When you have this healthy relationship within the family, you can be confident in talking about your teenage life in general because you know what a healthy and respectful relationship looks like at the start and can relate this to romantic relationships. When you can have a comfortable conversation with your parents, talking about romantic and sexual teenage relationships will be like talking about friendships or anything in school or daily life. Therefore, keeping the line of communication open with your parents is an excellent way to live your life as a teenager.

Being in a relationship in adolescence can help boost your confidence, and you will discover that you are happier when the connection is characterized by good communication and intimacy. Young people value the trust, support, and closeness they experience while in a romantic relationship (Act Youth, n.d.).

However, regardless of how perfect your relationship seems, it also has its downsides, like the inevitable breakups. Entering into a relationship at a very early age leads to your emotional vulnerability when experiencing breaking up. You are more sensitive to rejection when you're young, and breaking up can trigger despair and self-doubt. Once you experience having a low-quality relationship characterized by lack of trust, dating violence, and constant bickering, you may develop anxiety and depression.

The relationship between depression and early dating is not entirely understood, but pre-teen dating is associated with depression, especially for girls when there is sex involved. Poor treatment by a partner and inequality within a relationship often leads to depression, although the source of emotional difficulty can likewise be from outside the relationship. Those very young girls who date early often come from struggling families and may start with a relationship that is vulnerable to depression. This shows that there is evidence that depression leads young girls to seek relationships early.

Appropriate Relationships

When you date someone two years or more older than you, there is always this tendency to have an unequal relationship where one is usually not respected by the other. You will also have a higher chance of having sex and unintended pregnancy.

Having a relationship with someone before reaching the age of consent is against the law.

The age of consent usually varies in each state and ranges from 15-to 18 years old, although some states have close-in-age exemptions.

Even if the teens make the first move, look or act mature, or give permission, they are considered underage.

What Are Healthy Relationships are Like?

Healthy relationships have certain characteristics that you must learn, including:

Good Communication

Learn to communicate honestly and openly. Remember that communication is a two-way process and it also involves listening and allowing others to speak for themselves.

Mutual Respect

This pertains to identifying the values of another person and respecting their boundaries.

Trust

Learning to trust people you love and care for and giving each other the benefit of the doubt.

Fairness

Even in conflict, you must learn how to fight fairly. Avoid hitting below the belt and avoid being subjective.

Honesty

Honesty is the foundation of trust and helps strengthen a relationship. Without honesty in one or both parties, the relationship will suffer and ultimately end up in separation.

Equality

There must be equality in a relationship. Most often, girls and women suffer most in an unhealthy relationship because of inequality. This is where drawing boundaries is important to ensure equality in your relationship.

Compromise

Even when in a relationship, you still have your individuality to maintain. Neither of you need to compromise who you are as you need not forgo your identity for your partner. You and your partner should continue engaging with your own set of friends and doing things you love. Instead of giving up your interest or asking your partner to stop doing what they want, support each other, whether it be in pursuing new interests and hobbies or making new friends.

Forgiveness

It's not easy to forgive or forget. But if you want your relationship to survive, you must learn from past mistakes. This is not only applicable to romantic relationships, but also to other relationships like sibling-sibling, parent-child, and even to your relationship with long-time friends. It is said that a close and long-term relationship hurts most, but love and care will teach you to forgive and forget.

Mutual Giving and Receiving

A relationship is always two-way, like communication. It's a give-and-take. It's why it is a partnership and not one taking advantage of the other. If there is manipulation or exploitation, your relationship is not healthy and will end in a struggle for the one on the losing end.

Openness With Each Other

Love's basic foundation is trust, and loss of trust happens when betrayal comes in between two people in a relationship. To avoid this, there must be no secrets between you and your partner. Remember that no secret will remain in hiding forever. Sooner or later, any secret you or your partner keep will surface, and you know what will happen to your relationship. When such a thing occurs, pride will arise, and that's what triggers more negative emotions that usually lead to separation in a relationship.

Supporting Each Other

Each must be supportive of their partner when they want to pursue something new like a shift in career, a new hobby, or new friends.

Separate Identities

It's best to retain your identity and not conform completely to that of your partner. You should maintain your own set of friends and do things you love. Each of us still has our identity regardless of the relationship that binds us to each other.

Boundaries

It helps to draw your boundary lines at the start of every relationship, so it's clear for everyone. A healthy relationship must include boundaries to prevent one partner from getting over the fence. This is very important for teens, especially girls. From the very start, make it clear to your partner that sex is out of the picture, not until you're both at the right age and time.

Anger Control

There's nothing wrong with getting angry. However, you should check yourself and not allow your anger to affect the relationship. Why not take a few deep breaths before unleashing your anger on your partner. You may even choose to get away from a situation for a few hours to cool down before discussing the issue with your partner. It always pays to have a cool head.

Unhealthy Relationships

Nobody's relationship is perfect because no one is perfect and people make mistakes. But if you feel like you're in a relationship where your partner treats you badly, then you probably are. Always listen to what your gut tells you if you don't want to listen to other people. Remember that healthy relationships make you feel good about yourself while unhealthy relationships don't.

Unhealthy or abusive relationships can lead to severe consequences, including injury, long-term emotional trauma, and even death.

Mean, disrespectful, controlling, or abusive behavior. A controlling partner makes all the decisions for you — not giving you a chance to exercise your right to decide what to wear, where to go, what to do, and who to go with. A control freak is unreasonably jealous most of the time and will try to isolate you from your family and friends.

Codependence. It is unhealthy when you or your partner feels that you can't live without others. In this case, the codependent one may do something drastic when threatened or when the relationship ends.

One-sidedness. Your partners may be too narrow-minded to listen or accept reasons in an argument, conflicts, or disagreements that may arise anytime.

Dishonesty. One of the partners may resort to lying or keeping a secret. It also results in distrust.

Cheating. One of you could be cheating which may lead to a loss of trust and confidence.

Put down in public and private. It equates to a loss of respect when your partner makes fun of you in public or even in private.

Threats. Threatening is also a form of control when your partner tries to make you fearful and timid. They may threaten you with breakup or violence or attempt to keep you away from family and friends.

Pressuring you to change who you are or to do things you don't want to do. You have a partner who makes all the decisions and expects you to do everything they want — like what to wear or do with your life. This person is often unreasonably jealous and keeps you away from your friends and family.

Some Signs of an Abusive Relationship

Relationships vary, and so do the signs of an abusive relationship. However, all of these behaviors are ways that one of the partners tries to maintain all of the power and control in a relationship.

Sometimes, abusive behaviors gradually surface but get worse as time goes on. Therefore, if you feel devalued, controlled, and afraid most of the time, it's time to get out of the unhealthy relationship and get help. Everyone, regardless of age, deserves to be in a relationship where you and your partner feel safe, respected, and loved.

Learn to spot signs of an abusive relationship.

- ◆ Your partner always controls you and keeps tabs on your whereabouts and activities.
- ◆ They try to isolate you - away from friends and family.
- ◆ Use of verbal insults, mean language, and nasty put-downs
- ◆ Hitting, slapping, and other physical abuses
- ◆ Forcing you into sex
- ◆ You always feel bad about yourself

How to Cope an Unhealthy Relationship

When in an unhealthy relationship, inform a trusted friend or family member of what is going on in your life and make sure that you are safe. Don't attempt to make excuses or misinterpret violence, possessiveness, or anger as an expression of love. Justifying these actions will only worsen the situation. Even if the person hurting you loves you, their actions aren't justifiable and it's unhealthy for a relationship.

No one deserves to be hurt, hit, shoved, or forced into anything they don't want to do.

When in an abusive relationship, take note that you aren't alone. Also, you deserve better than where you are. When your partner hurts you—either sexually, physically, or tortures you mentally—nothing can justify what they're doing to you. We can get mad from time to time, but we can always talk things through to deal with the issues—not by hurting or putting our partner down.

Abuse happens not because you did something terrible. It happens because you failed to implement some preventive measures to prevent the abuse from happening. Abuse, especially domestic abuse, happens because one partner manipulates and controls the other partner to prove they are in control. But, don't forget that you all deserve to be happy, and it can only happen in a healthy relationship. Regardless of what form, abuse is a sign of an unhealthy relationship, and when you are in it, you have to get out as soon as possible.

When breaking up with an abusive partner, it is vital to have a safety plan if you feel they will hurt you and your loved ones. For support and advice, check out the safety plan of the National Domestic Violence Hotline at 1-800-799 SAFE (7233). If you're in immediate danger, get away from your partner and contact 911.

Dos and Don'ts in Relationships

Before you go out dating, you must learn about the value of respect and the characteristics of healthy and unhealthy relationships. You may not be equipped with the necessary skills to develop and maintain healthy relationships, and you may not know how to break up when needed appropriately. Keeping open lines of communication will help you form healthy relationships, quickly recognize the signs of unhealthy relationships, and prevent violence before it even starts.

Being comfortable means:

- You feel free and confident about yourself around the other person.
- You may disagree with them but know that it's all right. You can trust each other even when you're away from each other.
- You don't control each other by forcing the other person to do things against their will.

Don't Stay Away From Friends

There are people whose life revolves only around the person they're dating. It means dropping friends that have been with them before the relationship began. They may not intend to do this, but then it happens. If you were in your friend's shoes, would you be happy to have a friend who threw you over for someone else? Remember that outside your romantic relationship, you still have your social life.

Do Be Your Own Person

It's natural to share an interest with the person you're interested in, but take note that you need to maintain and develop your own identity. You still have your own personal likes and needs and interests. Maintaining your own identity apart from your partner will improve your self-esteem and confidence in the relationship.

Don't Hide From Issues

If you get into any relationship issue, don't panic. When it happens, it doesn't mean the end of your relationship. But if you choose to hide from the problem, it will grow. So before it does, admit when something is wrong and talk about it. It helps to fix it together instead of trying to ignore it or hide from the issue.

Sometimes it can be awkward or scary, but it's worth facing the issue, and it will get easier. Working through any problem in your relationship is a part of any good and healthy relationship.

Identifying Good Against Bad Conflicts

We tend to see conflict in a bad light, but that's not always the case. Sometimes, problems can bring you and your partner closer together if you can stick to the following rules during a disagreement.

Handling Conflicts and Difficulties in Relationships

Conflicts are inevitable in every relationship, and arguments aren't necessarily a bad sign. It simply means differences are surfacing because people are different, and their desires and needs will inevitably clash. Resolving disagreements develops healthily understanding and brings couples closer. The goal is to improve the relationship. We consider this a positive conflict.

There are relationships where differences aren't acknowledged due to the following reasons:

- ♦ One partner is in control of the relationship.
- ♦ Both individuals are merged and don't know themselves.
- ♦ Both are sacrificing who they are to please one another.

These solutions to differences backfire because the couple eventually builds up passive-aggressive behavior and resentment, which affects their intimacy and closeness. For some couples, conflict can be a sign of growth and maturity. Still, in the end, differences between high-conflict teams can escalate into power struggles, and communication can turn aggressive.

What to do During a Conflict

It is crucial to verbalize your needs and wants in a positive conflict and mutually work out compromises. How you approach your differences and intentions is critical to resolving your conflict. The goal is to resolve the dispute to the satisfaction of both parties. It's not about winning. You may come out the winner in the argument, but the relationship may suffer if your partner feels wounded and resentful even after meeting halfway.

Planning is significant for a satisfactory result when, where, and how you approach a disagreement. Therefore, it helps to make the rules of engagement in advance. Here are some suggestions to consider. You are not expected to achieve all of them, but it's always good to try.

- ◆ Make it okay to agree to disagree.

- ◆ Work through things as they come up. Don't stockpile resentments.

- ◆ Separate the person you care about from the behavior.

- ◆ Take responsibility for your needs, emotions, and behavior. When sharing your thoughts and feelings, use "I" statements instead of "You."

- ◆ Examine what unmet needs are making you angry.

- ◆ Brainstorm solutions rather than demanding your way.

- Communicate your guilt and fears in the relationship.

- Avoid making accusations and bringing up the past.

- Don't expect your partner to read your mind.

Cheating

We all have different opinions about cheating. You and your partner should decide what cheating means to you both in your relationship.

Here are some ways to tell if something you're doing might count as cheating:

- You hide something or lie about what you did.

- You did something you know your partner will be upset about when they find out.

- You feel guilty about what you did.

- You wouldn't want your partner to do what you did.

If you're always thinking about cheating or want to cheat, it could be a sign that you don't want to be in your relationship. Although breaking up with your partner sucks, it's less painful than cheating on them behind their back.

Breaking Up and Move On

Breakups and broken hearts are part of teenage relationships.

Teens typically have shorter relationships because adolescence is when you instinctively see lots of different experiences and try out other things. The things you want out of a romantic relationship change as you grow older.

Maintaining a bad relationship that you don't want to be in will be unhealthy for you and your partner. It's unfair to your partner to be in a relationship when you're not into it. The longer you wait to end it, the more it will hurt. So, it's better to be honest, and take action as soon as possible, even if you find it hard to initiate the breakup.

It is expected that you will feel sad and emotional once you end a relationship. However, this experience will teach you to cope with difficult situations and disappointments. You may want to share how you feel with a close friend or family.

There are things you shouldn't do, here are some of them.

♦ Avenge yourself through gossiping, bullying, revealing secrets between the two of you, etc.

♦ Look for a rebound relationships.

♦ Pretend you're okay and try your best to hide your feelings.

Breaking Up With Someone

Breaking up with your partner can be as hard as being dumped yourself. You may worry about hurting them and feel sad about the breakup even when you know it is the right thing to do. You can make your breakup suck less by being straightforward and honest about your feelings while trying to be as kind and compassionate as possible.

If you're unsure what to say, try writing down what you feel and your reasons for the breakup. You may also seek the advice of friends and family members.

You may say things like, "You're a great person, but I don't think we're right for each other," or "I like you a lot, but I don't feel ready to be in a relationship."

You don't need to be specific, but neither is it a good idea to lie or make up something to make them feel better. Acting rude or distant, as well as ghosting, are also uncool ways to end a relationship. It may not be ideal to break up with someone, but continuing in the relationship when you're no longer interested is cruel.

Moving On From a Relationship

It's hard to lose your first love, and it isn't something you're emotionally prepared to cope with. It can help have family members and close friends to lean on when you do. To cope with the heartaches, talk with someone who cares about you and is willing to listen and help. Friends can be a great source of comfort. Also, don't forget your parents. If you have open communication with your parents, they're the best people to ask for support.

It's totally normal and all right to be sad after a breakup, but if your sadness affects your grades, activities, and relationships with family and friends, think about talking to a therapist or counselor.

It is normal to be anxious or get angry after a breakup, especially if your relationship lasted for several years and you get used to having them around. But keep from posting about it on social media. It will only lead to a drama that can end up embarrassing you. Remember that something posted online will remain forever. Even when deleted, there will be copies of those posts somewhere else. If you're feeling super angry and hurt, find someone to vent to privately. It also helps to do something physical or creative, like involving yourself in a new hobby or sport. These will help you work through your emotions.

Some people try to stay friends with their ex, but it can be challenging to transform your romantic relationship into a friendship, and it's not a good idea to hook up with your ex after your breakup.

It's alright to get away from your ex in real life and on social media. It means unfriending and unfollowing them for a while or until you can get over the relationship.

Some try healing by getting into a rebound relationship. You may feel better for the moment, but this may be unfair to your new partner if you still have feelings for your ex. Better wait for your heartache to heal before looking for a new relationship.

CHAPTER 4

LET'S TALK ABOUT SEX

The Centers for Disease Control and Prevention (CDC) released a report which claimed that over half of the U.S. teens experienced intercourse by the age of 18 (Center for Disease Control and Prevention, 2018).

Sex is an exciting topic for teenagers, and there's nothing wrong with being curious about it. As a teenager, you go through puberty when your hormones significantly affect your body and emotions in various ways.

The changes you go through during this stage result in your interest in sex and having someone you are sexually attracted to. By sexual attraction, you begin to develop sexual thoughts, feelings, and body sensations. You might start to think about how sexy this particular person is and how you want to kiss them—this is sexual attraction. Again, I have to emphasize that these are normal for anyone in their teens.

However, you must understand that there are consequences to every little thing we do, and sex is not an exception. Before you decide to engage in any sexual activity, it is wise to learn essential things in line with this subject matter.

Limitations of Sex Education in Schools

The Centers for Disease Control and Prevention reports that about 55% of teenagers have already committed the act of sexual intercourse by age 18. However, Guttmacher Institute says teens receive less sex education than before. With the increase in sexual activities among teens but the decrease in formal sex education, we can only expect a spike in adverse consequences (e.g., unwanted teen pregnancies, STDs among adolescents, and increased HIV/AIDS cases) (Guttmacher Institute, 2016).

It is a dire situation.

However, government officials, educators, and parents in many parts of the world hesitate to incorporate or develop a curriculum for sex education. The reason for this is that they still believe this might promote sexual promiscuity among teens.

In reality, no study can back up that sexual and reproductive health education and information will lead to the rise of sexual activity among adolescents. Many teenagers still engage in sexual activities despite the restrictions adults impose.

Teenagers like you have the right to access quality sex education because it affects their overall health and well-being. If truth be told, comprehensive sex education classes have been proven to minimize misinformation about sex. Furthermore, it equips young people to make sound decisions about their health.

It is unfortunate and unacceptable that schools limit this aspect of practical education, leaving teens more vulnerable.

There are also instances wherein religion and culture play a vital role in why teens have difficulty in obtaining education about sex. Take the concept of "the birds and the bees," wherein adults tend to sugarcoat the truth about sexual reproduction. We don't even have to mention the lack of medically accurate information and curriculum development to include LGBTQ+ identities.

Fortunately, there are institutions and reliable online tools that can fill the gap our formal education providers have left. And it is good that you have this book to introduce you to valuable information about what you need to know about sex.

Why Do You Need to Learn About Sex?

Sex education is designed to aid adolescents in obtaining accurate information and practical skills needed to make the best choices for themselves about sex and relationships, which they can use in their lifetime.

Through sex education, young people learn to have healthy relationships and support disempowered individuals. Most importantly, they learn to love and prioritize themselves.

Sex education, especially when culturally comprehensive and responsive, allows young people to develop better emotional and social skills. It leads them to grow as compassionate and empathetic adults in the future. Adolescents who learn from this type of sexual education are more open-minded and can:

- Prevent dating or getting intimate with a toxic individual
- Appreciate sexual diversity
- Build strong connections and develop healthy relationships
- Experience improved emotional and social learning.
- Increase their media literacy
- Prevent child sex abuse
- Avoid sexually transmitted diseases or infections and unplanned pregnancies.

Sex education is effective when it is:
- Taught by skilled professionals (e.g., trained teachers or sex educators)
- Taught early and regularly throughout one's lifetime
- Evidence and trauma-informed
- Includes LGBTQ+ welfare
- Involves both information and skill-building activities
- Does not condone racist practices

♦ Tailored to the needs of the community

Why Do People Have Sex?

Humans are wired for sex; our brains are programmed to drive us toward this behavior. So, when you ask why people have sex, you are requesting something that goes like, "Why do you eat (or drink)?" or "Why do you sleep?"

There are hundreds of reasons why people have sex, but they are categorized into four main groups:

♦ Goal-based motivation: For procreation, revenge, or to improve social status.

♦ Emotional motivation: Because of love, gratitude, and commitment.

♦ Physical motivation: To satisfy sexual curiosity or because of attraction; it could also be for pleasure, exercise, and stress relief.

♦ Insecurity reasons: Because of pressure or a sense of duty; to boost self-esteem or prevent your sexual partner from seeking sex somewhere else.

Many find the following popular reasons for having sex:

- Sexual curiosity
- Peer pressure
- Pleasure
- Boost mood or relieve stress
- Boost self-esteem
- Make money
- Procreation
- Partner novelty
- Improve reputation or climb the social ladder
- Filling the need for affection
- Feeling loved by a partner or showing love to them
- Duty
- Jealousy
- Revenge
- Spiritual transcendence

You also have to consider the difference between the sexes. In general, men seek sex for the sake of pleasure. Women tend to "do" it because they are more interested in developing a relationship—of course, this doesn't mean that they don't feel pleasure during intercourse.

Experts describe these differences as person-centered and body-centered sex.

Person-centered sex is when you commit the act of intercourse to establish a connection with your sexual partner. You deeply care about the emotions involved in your relationship. And for those whose reason is to connect with their sexual partners, this act isn't merely "sex" but "love-making."

On the other hand, body-centered sex is when you have sex simply because doing it is pleasurable, or it might be because that is how you feel in the "heat" of the moment.

Men usually start out being body-centered but change eventually, especially as they age. Women tend to become more like men over time. They believe that sex is all about connection and developing, nourishing, and maintaining relationships at first. Later on, they would focus on pleasure since their relationships with their partners have progressed.

Yet, I must emphasize that we cannot easily dismiss that men are body-centered and women are person-centered. Some men believe that there should be an emotional attachment first before having sex with a partner. Likewise, some women have sex out of pleasure.

Should You Have Sex?

Most health experts advise that teens avoid having sex because it causes emotional and physical problems. Others claimed abstinence is the only safe sex. After all, it bears the truth since having no sex means you cannot expose yourself to health risks and unintended pregnancies.

Your parents cannot supervise you 24/7, and young people your age tend to rebel the more they feel restricted.

So, just a little precaution before you decide to be intimate with your girlfriend or boyfriend—understand that having sex comes with multiple responsibilities. And those responsibilities do not begin and end when you wear condoms or take birth control pills. You have to consider a lot of things such as:

Personal values: Do you believe that you should trust your partner first before having sex with them? Do you prioritize education first before anything else?

Maybe you believe in marriage first before having sexual intercourse?

Family values: What does your family think about dating and sexuality? Does your parents' opinion matter when it comes to your decision-making? Does your family adhere to graduation first before a committed relationship?

Religious beliefs: What do you think about abstinence? Do you believe that premarital sex is a sin? What is your opinion about the principle behind marriage before sex?

Emotional preparedness: Do you believe that you are ready to do it? Do you feel reluctant, perhaps? Do you feel pressured or coerced?

Teenagers may have different reasons why they want to lose their virginity, and these include:

- Curiosity
- Believing that they are in love
- Pressure from peers or partner
- Seek attention and affection
- Media and social media influence
- Rebellion

However, sex should NEVER be forced on you regardless of your gender. Likewise, it helps if you are never pressured into losing your virginity for any reason.

When you observe the following indicators, you will realize that your relationship is not yet ready for sex.

◆ Your lover is manipulative. (For example, they bully you or threaten to leave you when you disagree with what they want.)

◆ They are jealous and possessive. (For instance, constantly checking your phone messages, preventing you from spending time with friends or loved ones, and getting mad whenever they see you talking with someone else.)

◆ They pressure you to have sex even if it is against your convictions.

Why Wait?

Deciding whether it is all right for you to have sex is one of the most crucial decisions you will have to make. Remember that everything has its timing, and sharing intimacy with the right person has its own.

You must be emotionally mature enough to manage the consequences of having sex. It is wise to delay it as long as possible taking these points into consideration.

Let me give you more reasons why procrastinating to have sex is reasonable:

- Sex can result in out-of-wedlock pregnancy and birth.
- Sex exposes you to various health perils, such as STDs or STIs.
- Sex can bring about distractions, emotional pain, and depression.
- You can enjoy being a teenager without minding the consequences mentioned above.
- Having sex during your teens might be illegal where you live.

When Are You Ready for Sex?

Because everyone is different and not all relationships are the same, there can't be a standard answer to this question. It would be appropriate to start being sexually active with your partner in a relationship once intimacy, commitment, and passion are established and when both of you have pretty equal amounts of these feelings for each other.

Sex is a life-changer and can affect how other people see or feel about you and how you see yourself. Deciding if you are ready to have sexual intercourse with your lover is a huge decision and very personal.

Despite how the media portrays teens nowadays, many teenagers still believe that waiting until they are ready to have sex is important. Some want to hold back until their relationship is ready or until they are adults who can handle a relationship better.

You may feel that your relationship can go to the next level when:

- ◆ You and your partner can trust each other.
- ◆ You can talk to each other about personal matters without feeling judged, like relationships, feelings, and risks.
- ◆ You can discuss complex topics such as whether you had STI or had been pregnant (or impregnated one) before.
- ◆ You respect each other's decisions about having or not having sex.
- ◆ You learned how to use birth control and have safe and protected sex.

♦ You are fully aware of the consequences of having sex.

To help you with this, here's a sample checklist for readiness to have sex:

♦ Do you feel safe with your partner?

♦ Do you feel pressured to have sex? Does your partner pressure you?

♦ Did you and your partner honestly discuss sex?

♦ What do you expect from a sexual experience?

♦ Can you identify the risks linked with having sexual intercourse?

♦ Do you know what constitutes statutory rape in your country or state?

♦ What form of contraception do you consider using?

♦ Have you and your partner been checked for STIs or STDs?

♦ Were you able to talk about the possibility of pregnancy?

♦ Are you ready to raise a child? Would you consider abortion if you became pregnant (or impregnated your girlfriend)?

At the same time, do not be harsh on yourself if you had "done" it with your special someone and later realized you should not have. Furthermore, know that just because you had one-time sex with someone does not mean that you have to continue to do so. You have the power to say "yes" or "no" regardless of anyone else's opinion.

Your relationship is not ready for sex if you can see these signs:

- ♦ Your partner is too possessive, like constantly check your cellphone or calling you when you're in school or at work.

- ♦ The partner pressures you to go to bed with them and refuses to see your point of view.

- ♦ Your partner is either trying to manipulate you through bullying or threatening to hurt themself when you want to end the relationship.

Wrong Reasons to Have Sex

Sometimes, people only want to prove themselves to the point of doing the wrong things. This desire can be overpowering, especially in teenagers. For this reason, many decide to lose their virginity and join the pool of the "experienced" ones.

Perhaps, you are facing this kind of pressure now. Your reason for wanting to be sexually active may be in the list below. So, I hope you will spare some time to reconsider before finalizing your decision.

"I'm already a grown-up now."

You may have physically matured and become more independent, making you feel you're ready to bring the relationship with your special someone to another level. However, you still have more growing up to do emotionally. Even fully grown adults still have room for emotional development. Being an adult also means dealing with numerous sex-related responsibilities. What do you think those responsibilities are? Do you believe that you can already handle them?

"They say sex is enjoyable, so I'm up for it!"

Many teenagers live by the YOLO (You Only Live Once) philosophy. It makes them forget about the long-term consequences of their actions. They enjoy the physical and emotional gratification sex provides, but they overlook its life-changing effects.

Sex might provide you with short-term enjoyment, but it can create serious repercussions. Have you thought about these? Remember that there are numerous ways to create fun memories and build a connection with your special someone without engaging in sexual activities.

"Everybody's doing it, so why shouldn't I?"

People, not only teens, tend to think this way: The more people do it, the more it's accepted. But this does not always happen and should never be applied when it comes to something as serious as the issue of sex.

"Sex can draw me and my special someone closer."

Many teenagers, particularly girls, mistakenly believe that offering their bodies and virginity to their sweethearts can make that person stay. Others say that it's the best way to show their partner they love them. Sadly, these beliefs are detrimental to their physical and psychological health.

Nobody should feel pressured to have sex to reassure themselves or the other person of their love.

Likewise, pressuring someone is never okay, and it can be a red flag in an abusive relationship.

Sex is a unique way of sharing love with your special someone, and it requires mutual respect. A relationship that couldn't stand because there is no sex involved lacks genuine love. Moreover, there are many ways to share love without the involvement of sex.

"Other people had sex early in life, so why can't I?"

What you are saying might be a fact. However, you might not have heard the entire story of the people you are talking about and have missed the part about how they handled the consequences of their actions. If the people you are referring to are your parents, why not have a heart-to-heart talk with them? They could share their wisdom based on experience and help you decide.

"My friends will like me more if I have sex."

Let me ask you this straightforwardly— Would they still like you if you got pregnant or had a sexually transmitted disease? Would they remain your friends if things went wrong?

It is wrong to believe that having sex or sleeping around will make you a cool kid. If you want to be a famous individual on your campus, you can be the cool, smart one or the cool yet warm-hearted idol. You can be admired for countless reasons without being famous for sexual exploits.

To have sex or not should be your decision, and you shouldn't be forced, pressured, or manipulated into it. In the following chapter, we will further discuss the concept of consent.

It's not wrong to wait when it comes to sex. Don't believe it when they say that everyone is having sex because half of all teens in America have never had sex. So, once you decide to wait, stick to your decision and don't be swayed regardless of how much you love your partner. Plan how you can gracefully reject him or her without hurting their ego. What is important is they should clearly understand your reasons for saying NO. Also, stay away from situations that can lead you to sex.

It makes sense to wait for the following reasons:

Sex can lead to early pregnancy

Are you ready to be a child-parent? It is a big responsibility for you. Can you provide your baby with food, clothing, education, and a secure place to live?

Sex exposes you to health risks

A lot of infections can be spread when you indulge in sex. Sexually Transmitted Infections (STIs) include contagious diseases like gonorrhea, AIDS, syphilis, herpes, HIV, chlamydia, hepatitis B, and human pappilomavirus (HPV).

Sex can result in emotional pain and distractions

It can be irritating when someone pressures you to do things, like have sex, when you don't want to do it especially when your partner chooses to break up with you just because you did not agree to go to bed with them. They may even spread rumors about you to save their pride.

How Teens Can Resist Sexual Pressure

Teens are more likely to be active in sex if they:

- Entered the puberty stage early
- Engage with teens who approve of and encourage sexual activities
- Have a poor relationship with parents, particularly with their fathers
- Place little value on education
- Seldom attend religious services

Teens who have sex before they are ready usually regret it. Indeed, you don't want that to happen to you. Isn't WAITING better than REGRETTING?

However, we also know that the pressure on you to have sex is enormous. You have to contend with the direct pressure to do it with your date or steady boyfriend or girlfriend. There is also the peer pressure applied by friends who want to know if you did it. You may also feel the internal pressure to keep pace with your friends as if you're in a competition with your friends in a marathon to lose your virginity.

To fend off unwanted advances, consider the following:

Hook: Aw, come on, it's normal to have sex nowadays. Everybody does it!

Sinker: Who cares? I'm not everybody. Besides, not all are doing it, including those who say they do.

Hook: If you love me, you'd be willing to go to bed with me.

Sinker: If you love me, you won't pressure me to do it when I'm not yet ready.

Hook: If you're not prepared to have sex with me, it's better to breakup.

Sinker: If that's how you see it, better to split up.

Hook: Why don't you want to have sex?

Sinker: Because I don't want to, I don't think I need to explain it further.

Hook: We have done this before; why not now?

Sinker: Well, because I have the right to decide what to do with my mind and body. I can always change my mind, and I think it's better to do it when I'm old enough to take responsibility.

CHAPTER 5

YES, YOU MAY NOT!

H ave you ever been in uncomfortable situations of pressure to do something out of your will?

When you start dating and get into a relationship, you may experience something like this, especially concerning sex.

According to the study conducted by the Harvard Graduate School of Education, sexual assault rates among young people are high, and misogyny and sexual harassment appear to be pervasive among young people. Specific forms of gender-based violence are likewise increasing.

When teens are in a relationship, it can bring questions about intimacy and sex. Although not all of your relationships include sex, most of you are likely to experiment with sexual behavior at some stage (Raising Children Network, 2021).

Before you decide to have sex or become sexually active in any way, you need to know how to stay healthy. Here are some powerful reminders you should know and remember when in a relationship.

No one should be forced to have sex. If you are forced to do it, remember that it's never your fault, and you must not blame yourself. Instead, tell someone you trust as soon as possible, especially an adult— it could be your parent or teacher.

If you want to make a clear choice about sex, stay away from alcohol and drugs. Many young people get into sex without meaning to because they are on alcohol or drugs.

Sex and relationships can change your life—especially your relationships and future. Having it may change how you feel about yourself and how others may feel towards you.

Many teens still believe that waiting until they are ready for sex is essential, even at this age. You may want to wait until you become an adult or when you feel that your relationship is ready.

You can learn lessons for the future through early relationships. However, unhealthy relationships can lead to emotional and physical damage. Your first romantic relationship can be a good opportunity for you to understand what it means to be in a healthy relationship to have healthy, happy relationships throughout your life.

Don't wait until you're in a relationship before you learn what consent is all about and what's healthy or not healthy in a relationship. It's never too early to learn about healthy relationships. Most sexual experiences start with hook-ups which means sexual encounters without monogamy or commitments - compared to more traditional dating.

So when you're in a relationship, it's best to involve your parents. If you are close enough and have an open connection to seek their advice, you'll be better off. Your parents must know the person you are in a relationship with if both parents know each other. When your parents and your partner's parents are aware that their children are dating or in a relationship, you are more likely to wait to have sex until you're ready.

Consent

Consent is defined as asking permission to do anything sexual. You need to know that asking for consent is the first thing you ask for before touching anyone sexually. You also have to learn how to respect your partner's answer regardless of it being positive or negative.

Learning about consent will keep you and your partner safe and avoid hurting each other.

To learn about consent, start by making sure that you are familiar with what it means. Consent doesn't mean just because someone did not say, "NO!" It is not just implied but explicitly asked like, "Can I do...?" and the other party must communicate, "YES!" For consent to be executive, the person saying "YES" is not pressured, coerced, or forced into saying it; neither are they drunk or high.

Getting Consent

Consenting and asking for consent means that everyone is clear about their wants and needs — that partners are respecting each other's limits and boundaries. It's not right to pressure someone to engage in any sexual or romantic activity—or to go faster or further than they are ready for. Also, no one must pressure you to do the same. In short, consent should be:

Freely Given

When you freely give your consent, you make it without any pressure; neither are you manipulated nor were you under the influence of alcohol or drugs.

Reversible

Consent is reversible because you may change your mind about what you feel like doing. Even when you're both naked in bed or when you have done it before. You have the choice to stop or go on anytime you want.

Informed

You may only give your full consent if nothing is hidden from you. An example of this is when you consent to have sex if your partner will use a condom. If he disagrees, there isn't any consent on your part.

Enthusiastic

You are only considered to have given your consent when you want to have sex with your partner, not because your partner expects you to do it with them.

Specific

It must be apparent that you agree to do one and do not necessarily have to assume that you agree to what follows next. For example, you agree to go to the bedroom to make out. It does not necessarily mean that you agree to make out and arrange to have sex there.

You always have the final say about your body. Consent is never implied, and it is always clearly communicated. Silence is not giving consent, and whether you have had sex with the person before does not matter. You have to give your consent every time you have sex.

It is, therefore, illegal to do something sexual with someone who is not in their capacity to give consent, like when they are:

♦ Under the influence of alcohol or drugs

+ Asleep or passed out
+ They are younger than you or below the legal age of consent
+ Disabled - in a way that affects their ability to understand you

It isn't hard or awkward to ask for someone's consent. It even makes doing sexy stuff exciting and less awkward. Because when there's explicit consent, you also have a clear conscience. Knowing that the person you're with is down for doing the same thing you want takes the guilt away. Without asking first before you touch, kiss, or do anything sexual with someone, and they don't say yes, you don't have that person's consent, and what you're doing to them may be considered rape or sexual assault.

How to Ask for Consent

Consent is not just about what your partner is saying. It would be best if you also considered how they say it. If someone says yes, but their body language shows otherwise, it's time to slow down. Consent must offer affirmation in voice, tone, and body language. So when you observe hesitation or doubt, try to double-check or stop. Surely your partner would appreciate your action of taking their feelings into account. Going slowly and checking their boundaries won't hurt before moving forward.

If your partner is drugged or drunk, you have to stop. They might feel coerced if you go on while they're in such a state.

In the same way, you must stop when your partner does not actively consent to what you are doing. It can be considered rape or sexual assault.

When asking for consent, be explicit about it, like:

- Can I ... ?
- Do you want me to ... ?
- Should I keep going?
- How does this feel?
- What would you like me to do?

You must be direct when describing the act and wait until your partner responds. Always pay attention to your partner's body language and tone and frequently check-in with your partner to see if you're still on the same page.

Signs of Consent

Take note that your partner must give consent explicitly, and as your sexual encounter becomes more intimate, it needs to be given repeatedly. Also, notice that when permission is freely given, it must be indicated by a clear and excited "yes."

It is best to pay attention to your partner's reaction while getting their consent. Do they look happy or intimidated? If they don't appear happy and excited, you better stop.

Signs of Non-Consent

If your partner says "No!" or doesn't say anything, they aren't giving you their consent to proceed with the sexual act. If they answer "Yes!" but seem hesitant or uncomfortable, this also means that you DON'T have their permission and therefore have to STOP!

If you're unsure of what they want, check in before continuing. Check in by asking:

- To make sure that you want to do this, should I continue?
- If you're not into this, it's all right. We can do other things. What do you think?

The bottom line is not to pressure your partner to do something they are unsure about or don't want to do. Let them know that it's alright with you if they don't want to do it. Once it's clear that they don't like doing it, immediately stop asking them. Respect their boundaries so you can continue to have a healthy relationship. A controlling partner is a sign of an unhealthy and unsafe relationship.

Different people have different boundaries, so you must not hold it against them. Don't make them feel bad for saying NO; neither would you try to convince them that they're wrong and missing out on something they would have enjoyed.

How to Establish Boundaries

It's not easy to tell someone you love that you don't want to have sex with them. It is normal to worry because you don't want to disappoint your partner. However, you don't need to apologize or explain why. Saying NO or STOP is enough to show that you are drawing the line.

Make sure to draw your boundaries before anything else. Talk with your partner about your limits and wants.

You may say that it is against your personal beliefs or religion, so you don't feel like having premarital sex. Alternatively, you may consent to sex only if your partner uses a condom. Remind them that this safety measure is not only for you but also for them. You're both still too young for this responsibility, and your plans for the future are more important than having sex or early pregnancy.

Sexual Assault and Violence

Even when you have never experienced being harassed or bullied, you have probably witnessed or know someone who has. Especially now that smartphones and social media networks have become easy for bullies to harass their victims. When bullying involves sexual threats, advances, comments, or suggestions, it becomes sexual harassment.

Sexual harassment involves gestures, actions, comments, or attention intended to offend, intimidate, or hurt someone. Its focus is on the person's appearance, sexual orientation, activity, or body parts. It can be verbal but can likewise be unspoken. Bullies may harass you by sending inappropriate videos, text messages, or photos. Sometimes, it can get physical when someone tries to kiss or touch.

Sexual harassment is not limited to girls. It may also include boys as even girls harass boys, and boys harass other boys. It is not also limited to people of the same age group as adults who can harass teens and vice versa. But usually, teens are harassed by people in the same age group.

Sexual harassment and bullying are similar in that they both involve unwanted or unwelcome sexual comments, physical contact, and attention.

For examples:
- Spreading sexual rumors either in person, via text, or on social media.
- Showing someone inappropriate sexual pictures or videos.
- Shaming a person writing sexual messages on bathroom stalls or in other public places.
- Posting lewd videos, photos, or comments on Facebook and other social networks or sending explicit text messages.
- Asking someone to send you nude pictures of themselves.

- Proposing sexual offers while pretending to be someone else online.
- Touching, pinching, or grabbing someone deliberately in a sexual way.
- Brushing against someone or pulling at their clothes in a purposefully sexual way.
- Pestering someone by asking them to go out over and over again despite repeated denials.

Some things may be awkward but could not be considered harassment, like when a person suddenly swears using sex-related expressions out of surprise. But if a guy intentionally says sexual terms to a girl to make her uncomfortable, it can be sexual harassment. If you are not sure, you may ask yourself,

"Is this something I want to go on," or "How do I feel being subjected to all these?"

Handling Sexual Harassment

Bullies and manipulators are good at blaming others. So if you're being harassed, don't blame yourself, for no one has the right to harass or bully anyone else regardless of the situation sexually. It's not right to justify what they do by saying that you're asking for it.

There is no particular right way to respond to someone sexually harassing you. It can be helpful to tell that person to stop but that does not all the time. They may not listen to you and even laugh at you or bother you more.

It is better to share what's happening to you with an adult—either your parents, teacher, coach or anyone you can trust to help you.

Many schools today are addressing these issues of harassment and bullying. They are reassigning officers whom you can talk to about these issues.

It may be embarrassing to talk about sexual harassment at first, but your shyness wears off when you feel that someone is there and willing to listen and help you. Telling someone as soon as possible can lead to a fast resolution of the issues.

Having a record of the events can help. Make sure to write down important information like dates and short descriptions in a journal. Save offensive videos, photos, or text as evidence later if your school or family decides to take legal action against the bully.

If you witness someone being harassed, take action by speaking up against the harassment. Could you report it to a teacher or principal? It will help the victim and help eradicate bullies in your place if you do.

Sexual Violence

If you happen to be harassed or bullied in school, or it could also be the other way around, you have to talk to your parents. Being a bully will get you in trouble.

Bullies don't happen overnight. There is always a reason for this, so do not keep things from your parents. If you wait to tell someone about bullying things can get worse for you. You may be afraid of your parents, but there is more fear of bullies and the suffering endured by them.

But if you're experiencing bullying or sexual harassment, it can always lead to more significant troubles later if you continue to keep it to yourself. Bullied kids are also more likely to suffer because they will skip classes academically. Teens have even committed suicide because bullying can lead to depression and anxiety if not addressed early.

Rape or sexual assault is any undesired and forced sexual activity that happens without the person's consent. It is considered a criminal liability. It can include kissing and sexual penetration - vaginal, anal, or oral.

Sexual violence can happen even in a romantic relationship, between friends, family members, strangers, or acquaintances. Sometimes more than one person can commit sexual violence at a time, and anyone can be a victim.

Rape is forced on a victim, and sometimes the perpetrator uses drugs, physical strength, or threats to the victim who can't fight back.

Drugs commonly used are GHB, Rohypnol, and ketamine, mixed into drinks and not easy to detect.

Take note that even when both of you have sex while under the influence of alcohol or drugs, it can still be considered rape or sexual assault if there is no consent.

Protecting Yourself

To protect yourself from sexual assault:

♦ Avoid secluded places, especially when you're in the early stage of dating or just getting to know the person.

♦ Don't spend time alone with someone who makes you feel uncomfortable, and when you are with someone you can't trust, make sure to stay sober.

♦ Never drink something poured or opened, and be aware of your date's ability to agree to sex.

If you're a guy, you can be guilty of rape if the other person has been drinking or on drugs. There are many reported cases of guys getting trapped in marriage under these circumstances.

If possible, be clear about the kind of relationship you want with the person. As much as possible, go out with a group of friends and watch out for each other. It will also help if you take self-defense lessons.

What to Do if You Become a Victim

The first thing you do following a sexual assault is contact the police. However, deciding whether to report a rape or sexual assault to the police can be challenging, especially for teens. You will need the support of your parents or any adult you trust to decide and report the assault.

While still deciding, you may go to a hospital or doctor for medical attention as soon as possible. It is essential to reserve any evidence, so don't take a shower, wash, douche, or change clothes.

Have yourself tested for STD, pregnancy, or any injury.

As soon as you have decided to report it to the police, do so as quickly as possible. It is better to report the incident as soon as you can.

Write down as much as you can remember about the one whose mere presence makes you uncomfortable while you can still remember it clearly. Better yet, have someone take an audio or video recorder of you while narrating the incident.

Seek the help of a licensed counselor or therapist to guide you through any psychological treatment. It is one traumatic incident, and if left neglected, some psychological issues may later surface. If there's one thing that you need to bear in mind, what happened to you is NOT YOUR FAULT.

Many people, especially teens, think that it's their fault if the rapist is a family member, a friend, or someone they're dating. Regardless of who the perpetrator is, it's never your fault, even if you started doing something sexual with the person but didn't want to continue, and they forced their way. Also, what you're wearing or the way you're acting doesn't make it your fault.

Feeling safe again and being back to your old self may take time. However, it will help you talk to a therapist and connect with teens like yourself who have been through sexual assault.

Most areas have local hotlines and rape crisis centers to advise where to go for medical help. Calling on the assistance of the national sexual assault hotline at (800) 656-HOPE can be a great help as well.

CHAPTER 6

ACCIDENTS HAPPEN

S ex is a popular topic in entertainment, news, and advertising. It is a hard-to-avoid subject, so even young teens can see or hear about it everywhere. Many adults are reluctant to discuss it with young people despite its popularity.

Many parents still believe that sex is a sensitive topic for teenagers experiencing many changes in their bodies. They fear that bringing it up is akin to opening Pandora's Box. Unfortunately, parents who hesitate to educate their children about sex miss the right timing because of this kind of mentality. This factor contributes to why "accidents" happen.

Pregnancy

Once puberty begins, pregnancy becomes a considerable possibility. Teen pregnancy and childbearing is a life-changer. Both situations lead to substantial economic and social costs through immediate and continuing effects on teen parents and their children. It is particularly true for teenage girls who are scared, depressed, isolated, and cannot tell their parents about their current issues.

Pregnancy and childbirth are notable contributors to high school dropout rates among teenage girls. Only about 50% of teen moms tend to finish high school by age 22. Comparably, about 90% of teenage girls who did not become a mother in their teen years received their high school diploma. Meanwhile, teenage fathers are over 30% less likely to receive a high school diploma than other teenage boys (Center for Disease Control, 2021).

Children of teenage mothers are more likely to have lower academic achievements and a higher possibility of dropping out of high school. They also have more health problems, are prone to juvenile delinquency during adolescence, and face unemployement as young adults. This is because childbearing disrupts a teenage mother's development and introduces social and economic stressors that interfere with their ability to parent effectively. After childbirth, adolescent mothers are at risk for low educational attainment and single parenthood, which increase the likelihood that their children will be in a family environment marked by limited income and social resources. (Center for Disease and Control Prevention, 2021).

Pregnancy can be scary, especially for teens who can't tell their parents of their pregnancy. Feeling alone, scared, and isolated can pose a real problem.

Teen pregnancy is also connected to some health risks, some of which can be fatal, such as:

- Pre-eclampsia
- Pregnancy-induced hypertension
- Premature birth
- Low-birth-weight babies
- STDs or STIs
- Postpartum depression

Teenage fathers are also at risk of the following:

- Physical and mental stress
- Worries about their partner's and baby's health

- Financial difficulties
- Educational challenges
- Feelings of isolation and distress

While the surest way to avoid teen pregnancy is to abstain from sex, parents cannot force it on their teenagers. The second option is to learn how to use birth control methods of contraception to take every precaution to prevent pregnancy if you are having sex.

The most effective contraception for teens is long-acting reversible contraception (LARC). These include implants and intrauterine devices, which usually hold more than 99% efficacy. What is even better? They work for about three to ten years, and you can have them removed when you already want to start a family.

Suppose you opt for birth control pills, condoms, rhythm, or other types of contraception. In that case, you have to learn how to implement the method correctly. Discussing with your parents or guardian how to get birth control if you are already sexually active is a smart move. You can also ask the help of doctors or health care workers for guidance and prescription of birth control.

Sexually Transmitted Diseases (STDs)

Sexually transmitted diseases and infections are pretty frequent, and most people will have one at some point in their lives. In the United States, adolescents ages 15 to 24 are highly prone to STDs. About 50% of the new STD cases come from this age bracket each year. Because of this, it is wise for you to learn about safer sex before deciding to be sexually active (Center for Disease Control and Prevention, 2021).

Here are some of the crucial points to remember for safer sex:

♦ You are putting yourself at higher risk for STDs or STIs every time you engage in penetrative sex (i.e., anal, vaginal, or oral sex).

♦ You may think that kissing is safe, but it isn't. Through this activity, you can get or transmit herpes, syphilis, and CMV.

♦ You can spread STDs without knowing it. Some people may not experience immediate symptoms even when they have a sexually transmitted disease. And because of this, they can unknowingly give it to another person and cause them health problems.

♦ You should know that you do not need parental permission to get tested for STDs. You can always ask your local health center for assistance if you are worried about something.

Protecting Yourself

You should pair your decision to be sexually active with an equal action: protecting yourself. Practicing safe sex offers many advantages, with preventing unplanned pregnancy and being safe from STDs as the prime benefits.

Failing to take preventive measures means exposing yourself to the risk of acquiring STDs. The following are some of the common types of STDs disclosed and described by the Stanford Children's Organization (Stanford Children's Health, n.d.).

Chlamydia

Chlamydia, known as one of the most common STDs, can affect men and women. This particular disease can lead to severe and permanent damage to a woman's reproductive organs, making it hard for her to conceive. Additionally, chlamydia can also result in a fatal ectopic pregnancy (The Nemours Foundation, 2022).

Genital Herpes

Genital herpes is more common than you think. It is brought about by the herpes simplex virus (HSV) and can be transmitted and obtained through skin-to-skin or sexual contact and kissing.

People with genital herpes experience itching, pain, and sores in their genital area. However, it can also be possible to show no signs or symptoms. If a person gets infected with the virus, they can be contagious even without having visible open sores.

At present, there is no treatment yet for this disease. Still, some medications can alleviate its symptoms and lessen the risk of infecting others. Using condoms, for one, can help avoid the spread of this sexually transmitted disease (The Nemours Foundation, 2022).

Genital Warts (HPV)

Genital warts are typically found in the genital area. They are considered a sexually transmitted disease produced by the human papillomavirus (HPV).

These warts spread near the anus, cervix, penis, vulva, vagina, or scrotum. They can be of different sizes – small or large, flat or bumpy. In some cases, they are clustered together in a cauliflower-like shape.

The HPV that causes warts can be transmitted through anal, oral, vaginal, or skin-to-skin contact with the infected genital area. Sometimes, one can be infected but not have warts. Nevertheless, this does not mean they do not have an active HPV.

You can prevent genital warts and other HPV types by having an HPV shot. Using condoms during sex can also help — but not always — prevent the spread of this disease (Cleaveland Clinic, 2019).

Gonorrhea

Gonorrhea spreads through penetrative sex with someone infected with the virus. Someone who has experience:

- Lower belly pain and pain during urinating
- Rectal pain (especially when defecating)
- Pain in the testicles (males)
- Vaginal bleeding between periods
- Discharge from the penis, vagina, or anus

If left untreated, gonorrhea could cause damage to your reproductive system, preventing you from bearing or fathering a child later. You might also experience peeing problems because of scars in the urethra. There could also be blood infection, leading to joint problems (Center for Disease Control, 2022).

The best preventive measure against gonorrhea is sexual abstinence, but if it isn't your option, using or having your partner use a latex condom can help.

Hepatitis B (HBV)

Hepatitis B is a severe liver infection caused by the HBV or hepatitis B virus. For some, the infection can become a chronic condition. One can pass the virus through body fluids, blood, and semen to another person.

You may get or pass hepatitis B if you have unprotected sex since the virus is transmitted through saliva, blood, semen, or vaginal secretions. Pregnant women infected with the hepatitis B virus can also pass this to their babies during delivery. Fortunately, the newborn can be vaccinated to prevent getting infected.

Having hepatitis B increases the risk of developing liver cancer, liver cirrhosis, and liver failure. This condition is still untreatable, but getting vaccinated can prevent it from spreading to others (Center for Disease Control,2021).

HIV and AIDS

HIV, or human immunodeficiency virus, adversely impacts the immune system. When the immune system gets weaker, the body finds it difficult to fight off infections and certain cancers. Thankfully, people diagnosed early can take medicines for HIV, enabling them to live long, healthy lives.

AIDS or acquired immune deficiency syndrome can be developed when someone has had HIV for about eight to ten years. A person with AIDS has a severely debilitated immune system; thus, they experience serious health problems and infections.

You can get HIV when infected body fluids and blood enter your body, which can happen during vaginal or anal sex. HIV is brought down from mother to child during pregnancy, breastfeeding, and childbirth. It DOES NOT spread through:

- Holding hands
- Sharing eating utensils
- Sneezing and coughing

♦ Urine, excrement, saliva, sweat, or vomit

To minimize the risk of acquiring the virus, you should always practice safe vaginal, oral, or anal sex by using condoms during every sex act. Also, avoiding multiple sex partners will prevent spreading it. Get tested for HIV and ensure that all your partners do as well (The Nemours Foundation, 2022).

Pelvic Inflammatory Disease (PID)

This kind of disease is an infection of the female reproductive organs. It happens when bacteria get transmitted from a woman's vagina to their uterus, fallopian tubes, or ovaries through sex. Many bacteria cause PID, but chlamydia and gonorrhea infections are the most common.

To prevent PID, always use condoms during sex and limit the number of your sexual partners. Douching can also cause an imbalance of bacteria in your vagina, so avoid doing it (The Nemours Foundation, 2021).

Pubic Lice (Crabs)

Pubic lice are pinhead-sized insects that live in hair in the pubic region or near the genitals. They can also inhabit the eyebrows, eyelashes, and other body hair.

People with pubic lice experience itchiness, especially during nighttime. Lice bites can also result in skin irritation and redness.

Pubic lice or crabs can be transmitted and acquired through sex. However, they can also spread through infected bedding, clothing, and towels. It is implausible to get the lice from a toilet seat since it cannot live away from body warmth for long.

The best method to avoid lice is to abstain from having sex. Maintaining a monogamous relationship with a crab-free partner and practicing a rigorous grooming regime can also help. Condoms cannot protect you or your partner from pubic lice since they live where the condoms do not cover. Waxing or shaving cannot protect you from crabs (The Nemours Foundation, 2022).

Syphilis

Syphilis usually spreads by touching a chancre (sore) or lesions that look like warts called condyloma lata caused by syphilis. It typically happens through skin-to-skin contact or penetrative sex.

Symptoms of syphilis vary depending on its current stage. The stages are:

♦ Primary syphilis: one or multiple chancres

♦ Secondary syphilis: rash on palms and soles of the feet, flu-like symptoms, condyloma lata, hair loss, and swollen lymph nodes

♦ Latent syphilis: no apparent symptoms

♦ Late or tertiary syphilis: critical damage to the blood vessels, heart, nervous system, and other organs (The Nemours Foundation, 2018).

Trichomoniasis

Trichomoniasis, also known as trich, is caused by a parasite called Trichomonas vaginalis. Trichomoniasis can be passed on between men and women through vaginal sex. However, women can also spread this to other women through sexual contact. Men do not typically pass on trich to other men.

To prevent yourself from contracting trich, make sure that you (if you are a male) use a latex condom when having sex with a partner, although this isn't a foolproof method. If you are sexually active, it is best to get tested for STDs annually or more often (Mayo Clinic, 2022).

Birth Control or Contraception

Most teenagers who get pregnant did not plan it. While the most effective way to avoid unintended pregnancies is abstinence, this isn't the reality or the option for many teenagers nowadays. Hence, young people like you need to know and understand other birth control options to prevent facing this situation.

Condoms

Condoms are thin pouches that block the sperm from going into the vagina. There are condoms designed for both males or females.

Male condoms are worn on the penis. They are usually made of a type of rubber called latex. However, some are produced from polyisoprene or polyurethane, designed for those who are allergic to latex.

Female condoms (or internal condoms) are put inside the vagina. The close end goes inside while the ring end stays outside the opening of the vagina. They are usually made of synthetic latex or polyurethane.

Aside from accidental pregnancies, condoms made of polyisoprene or polyurethane protects you from STIs or STDs when used correctly, whereas latex condoms only help prevent STDs.

Using condoms in conjunction with other contraceptives for added protection is wise, such as birth control pills or IUDs. Note that condoms should not be reused and should be changed every time you have sex with your partner (The Nemours Foundation, 2022).

Intrauterine Devices (IUDs)

An IUD (Intrauterine Device), sometimes referred to as IUC (Intrauterine Contraception), is a mini device shaped like a T.

IUD is placed inside a female's uterus to prevent pregnancy. It is one of the most effective contraceptives since it has more than 99.9% efficacy. Meaning only one out of 100 women who use IUD can get pregnant.

There are two types of IUDs— hormonal and copper. Both prevent pregnancy by altering the way sperms move so that they cannot reach an egg.

Copper IUDs almost make it impossible for a sperm to reach an egg since sperm does not like copper.

IUDs also work exceptionally well as emergency contraception. If a female gets an IUD within five days (120 hours) after unprotected sex, the over 99% efficacy remains the same.

Unfortunately, IUDs cannot protect people from getting STIs or STDs. It is necessary to use other forms of protection like condoms to stay away from sexually transmitted diseases or infections (The Nemours Foundation, 2022).

Contraceptive Implants

Contraceptive implants can be used for an extended period to avoid pregnancy in women. It is a flexible plastic stick —roughly the size of a matchstick—that doctors or nurses insert on the skin of the upper arm. Women can be protected from pregnancy for up to five years, depending on the implant.

The implant releases a gradual yet steady dose of hormones that thickens cervical mucus and thins the endometrium or the uterus lining. It can also terminate ovulation, preventing pregnancy from happening. Out of 100 women who use an implant for a year, less than one can get pregnant. Meaning the implant's efficacy is more than 99.9%.

Contraceptive implants do not offer protection against STDs or STIs (The Nemours Foundation, 2022).

Contraceptive Injections

Contraceptive injections, also known as birth control shots, contain the hormone progestin. Progestin inhibits a woman's body from getting pregnant by making the cervical mucus thicker and suppressing ovulation.

To maximize the possibility of avoiding pregnancy, one has to take a shot every three months or 12 to 13 weeks. While contraceptive injections can hinder pregnancies, it is imperative to note that they cannot protect a person from sexually transmitted infections or diseases (The Nemours Foundation, 2022).

Birth Control Pills, Patches, and Rings

The birth control pill contains hormones and must be consumed daily. It triggers hormonal changes and controls a female's ovaries and uterus, resulting in pregnancy prevention.

Most birth control pills that inhibit ovulation by thickening the mucus around the cervix are a combination of pills. This process makes it hard for the sperm to enter the uterus and reach any released egg.

Birth control pills usually come in a 21 or 28-day pack. Women should take one pill every day at about the same time.

The birth control patch is a 4.5cm square pad that adheres to the skin. It releases pregnancy-obstructing hormones through the skin into the bloodstream, ultimately preventing ovulation.

The estrogen and progesterone hormones affect the uterus lining. For this reason, any fertilized egg will find it challenging to attach itself to the uterine wall.

Patches should be applied every week on about the same day to ensure their effectiveness. Let's say that the patch is first used on a Sunday, and then one has to apply it every Sunday.

The birth control ring is a circular device that can be inserted into a female's vagina. It gradually releases hormones through the vaginal wall into the bloodstream. The effect is just the same as when one uses birth control pills or patches.

To use the ring, a female has to put it into her vagina, similar to using a tampon. It should be inserted on the first day of the period and no later than the 5th day. If set correctly, the effectiveness of the birth control ring is more than 99% (The Nemours Foundation, 2022).

Cervical Cap

A cervical cap is a tiny cup made of soft silicone inserted deep inside a woman's vagina to cover her cervix. The cap stops the sperm from joining an egg. One must use the cup with a gel or cream that kills the sperms called spermicide. This way, you maximize the efficiency of this method.

Cervical caps are more effective for women who have never given birth. They have 86% efficacy, which means 14 out of 100 women can get pregnant in a year. Caps are only 71% effective for those who have already given birth. It means that 29 out of 100 can get pregnant within a year (Planned Parenthood, n.d.).

Like all contraceptives, the cervical cap is most effective when used correctly. Remember that following the instructions is crucial to making this work.

Diaphragm

A diaphragm is a form of contraceptive that looks like a shallow cup. The material used is soft silicone, making it flexible and comfortable. A woman has to bend it in half before inserting it into her vagina to use it.

A diaphragm acts as a barrier that shields the cervix, preventing the sperm from uniting with an egg. If you use a diaphragm, you must use it with spermicide to maximize its efficacy. Spermicide bears chemicals that hinder sperm cells from moving, making it almost impossible for them to join an egg (The Nemours Foundation, 2022).

Less Effective Birth Control

Note that the birth control methods listed below are less advantageous when used independently. In a year's time, over 20 out of 100 women who use these methods get pregnant.

Withdrawal

Withdrawal or pulling out is a birth control method wherein a male takes his penis out of the vagina before he ejaculates during sex. In doing so, he tries to prevent sperm from entering the vagina. However, this isn't a foolproof method to stop pregnancy. About 22 to 27 out of 100 couples who use the withdrawal method alone as birth control end up pregnant by the end of the year (Langmaid, 2016).

Rhythm Method

In the rhythm method, a woman learns to identify the days she is fertile and avoids engaging in sex the day before or during those days. It also involves monitoring vaginal discharge and changes in body temperature.

About 25% of women get accidentally pregnant each year using this method. However, it can be up to 90% successful if the rhythm is done correctly. Women who have regular menstrual cycles and are careful when they have sex can significantly benefit from this method (Cleveland Clinic, 2019).

Spermicides

Spermicides contain chemicals that prevent sperm cells from reaching an egg. However, to increase its efficacy, one should always use spermicides with other barrier methods such as cervical caps and diaphragms to boost its effectiveness.

Spermicides come in different forms, such as gels, creams, and foams. To apply, one should squirt it into the vagina using an applicator.

About 29 out of 100 women who use spermicide without other barrier methods get pregnant over a year (MyHealthAlberta & Healthwise Staff, 2021).

Protection from STIs or STDs

If you want to be safe from getting STIs or STDs, you should always avoid having intercourse with anyone with a rash, genital sores, discharge, or other symptoms. The only time unprotected sex is safe for you is if— and only IF— you and your partner practice mutual monogamy. Otherwise, you should strictly do the following:

- ♦ Do not forget to use latex condoms every time you have sex, especially penetrative sex. Use condoms throughout the duration of sex. Condoms may not be a guaranteed method of preventing pregnancy and STDs. Still, they can be exceptionally effective when used correctly.

♦ Wash before and after having sex.

♦ Do not share underwear and towels.

♦ Get a series of three-shot vaccination for hepatitis B.

♦ Get tested for HIV and at least yearly checkups for other STDs.

Many believed that using condoms with nonoxynol-9 helped prevent STIs or STDs before. However, a new study demonstrates that this can be a source of irritation in a woman's vagina or cervix, resulting in an increased risk of infection. Therefore, you should opt for condoms without nonoxynol-9 (Department of Health and Human Services, 2003).

Meanwhile, to avoid giving sexually transmitted diseases to someone else, you should:

♦ Use condoms whenever you have sex, particularly when you have a new sexual partner.

- Abstain from having sex until you get treated.

- Follow your doctor's instructions for treatment.

- Do not continue having sex unless you have your doctor's signal.

- Have a regular check-up, especially when you are sexually active.

- Make sure that your sex partner (or partners) gets treated.

Emergency Contraception (EC)

Emergency contraception is a method to avoid pregnancy after:

- Unprotected sex
- If the contraception used failed (e.g., the condom broke or missed taking the birth control pill)

There are two types of emergency contraception:

- Morning-after pill: can be taken up from three to five days (72 to 120 hours) after unprotected sex
- IUD (especially copper IUD): can be take up to five days (120 hours) after unprotected sex

145

Emergency contraceptive pills function by putting off a woman's ovulation. However, if fertilization and implantation have already occurred, emergency birth control pills will no longer impede the pregnancy.

Despite using ECs within 72 hours after unprotected sex, there is still a 1% to 2% chance for a woman to become pregnant. Moreover, women do not need to wait until "morning" to take the pill. It would be best to take it right after unprotected sex.

Emergency contraception will not hinder pregnancy if another unprotected sex happens after taking the ECs. Women should also remember that emergency contraception methods cannot prevent all pregnancies. They should visit their doctor in case of delayed periods.

Neither emergency contraception method can protect you against STIs or STDs. Always use condoms with birth control methods when having sex.

Some emergency pills are available over the counter in pharmacies and drugstores, while some will only be available with a prescription. Like the copper IUD, some contraceptives need to be inserted by a doctor or nurse in a medical facility.

Note that emergency contraception is not recommended for women who already know about their pregnancy and as a regular birth control method.

What if You or Your Partner Gets Pregnant?

Teenage pregnancy happens when a woman is 19 years old or younger. A woman who begun her monthly periods and engaged in vaginal sex with a man can get pregnant. In a 2020 survey by CDC, over 158,000 babies were born in the US to girls between ages 15 to 19 (Osterman et al., 2021).

While our medical technology certainly has been better than decades ago, giving birth during the teen years still poses a significant danger. In fact, WHO says that complications during pregnancy or childbirth top the list of causes of death-leading conditions among girls between ages 15 to 19 worldwide (World Health Organization, n.d.).

If you get pregnant (or your partner did), you might feel scared discussing it with your friends or family. Being unable to talk will only make you feel more isolated and depressed. These feelings can result in more issues in the home and at school.

Many pregnant teens leave school and never finish their education. It leads to numerous mothers who got pregnant in their teens living in poverty. Moreover, they are more likely to have multiple children. A woman with little education and several mouths to feed and care for will always find herself in a highly challenging situation.

While teen fathers might not have to worry about health hazards linked with pregnancy and childbirth, they could still face similar challenges in schooling and earning a living. Furthermore, he might be charged with statutory rape depending on the laws where he lives. It, of course, will produce devastating effects.

What Are Your Options?

Seeing a doctor usually frightens pregnant teens. However, you must remember that seeing one is crucial when in this condition. It is to ensure your safety and that of your child.

Your doctor should be able to talk with you about all available choices regarding your pregnancy. These options may include:

- Abortion: ending the pregnancy medically (i.e., in-clinic abortion or taking the abortion pill)

- Adoption: giving birth to your baby and legally giving the child to someone else

- Parenting: giving birth and raising your own child

Abortion

Deciding between abortion or having a baby is a very personal decision. However, there may be some valid reasons for having an abortion. Below are several reasons why pregnant teens decide to terminate their pregnancy:

- They are not ready to be a parent yet.

- They want to finish schooling and achieve their goals before having a child.

- They were victims of rape.

- They were in an abusive or illicit relationship.

- Their pregnancy could be life-threatening.

- The fetus has a slight chance for survival or will only suffer after birth.

If you have the intention of having an abortion, you should take time to consider these things first:

- Am I ready to be a parent? Or perhaps should I consider adoption?

- What do my personal or religious beliefs say about abortion? Do I deem it morally right or wrong?

- Am I just being pressured to get an abortion?

- Would having a child affect the way I want to live? How?

- Would having an abortion affect my way of life? How?

- What kind of support do I need when I decide on an abortion? How about when I choose to keep the baby?

- What would my future be if I had an abortion? How about when I keep my baby?

♦ Am I mentally prepared for the psychological impacts of an abortion?

You have numerous things to consider, and it is 100% normal for feelings and thoughts to get involved in your decision-making process. For this reason, it would be most helpful to obtain factual, unbiased information about abortion. And while the support from your loved ones can be beneficial, the decision is entirely yours to make.

Adoption

The adoption process involves that you choose someone else to parent your child. It is a legally permanent agreement wherein you agree to put the custody and care of your child to another person or family.

Again, whether you choose adoption for your child is ultimately your choice. Many couples from all over the world are hoping to build families through adoption. There are existing laws that will protect and guide you and the adopted families through the entire adoption process. Because of this, it is crucial to speak with an attorney or adoption agency regarding this matter.

In the United States, the adoption process is handled through public and private (or independent) portals and is open or closed.

- Private adoptions: The birth parents may work with a doctor, clergy, attorney, or licensed or unlicensed facilitator.

- Public adoptions: An agency contracted or operated by the state will designate the child to a family.

- Open adoptions: Allows birth parents to choose the adopted parents personally. They can meet with them and even maintain a lasting relationship.

- Closed adoptions: The names of both parties, the biological and adopted parents, are kept confidential from each other.

Before considering adoption as an option, there are many other things you have to bear in mind. To evaluate your situation, consider the following questions:

- Do I feel comfortable with the idea of adoption?

- Do I have the ability and means to raise a child now?

- Is someone pressuring me to put my baby up for adoption?

- Am I prepared to deal with the feelings of loss?

- Do I have people who will help me get through my pregnancy and adoption process?

- Do I believe that other people can take better care of my child than I can right now?

- Will I be okay with the thought that I might never see my child again?

Talking with your partner, parents, doctor, spiritual leader, or counselor will help you render a sound decision. It would be best to choose people you believe are uncritical and supportive of your situation.

Parenting

Parenting can be a rewarding, happy, and life-changing experience. Many parents of all ages say that it is one of the best decisions they have ever made in their entire life. However, having a child is also a life-long commitment. It will take you a great deal of energy, patience, and love to be a parent. Therefore, it is only natural to feel a wide range of emotions when deciding if you want to become a parent.

These questions will help enlighten you on whether you are ready to become one or you have to choose other options:

- Am I being pressured to become a parent?

- What does it mean to be a parent?

- Do I want to start my own family at this point?

- Can I handle the responsibilities of being a parent?

- Can I afford to take care of a child now?

- How would having a baby affect my future?

- Which should I consider, adoption or abortion?

- In what way will my partner and family support me?

- Will I feel comfortable parenting together with my partner?

- What would I think about co-parenting if we broke up?

- Could I handle being a single mom (or dad)?

Talking with the people you trust can lighten the load. You may likewise enlist the help of professionals, but you need to be careful in choosing "reliable" health centers. Ensure that you stay away from the so-called "Crisis Pregnancy Centers" that employ manipulative strategies to get pregnant women to delay actual medical care. The first red flag is that these centers do not have doctors, nurses, and other professional healthcare providers on their staff.

Keep in mind that nobody should force their decision on you. Deciding to become a parent is your personal choice. It is why talking with people who can provide you with hard facts and will not judge you should be a priority.

Misconceptions about Sex

Because sex is a hot topic among teens and adults alike, you can hear almost anything about it. The media and the people around you will always have a tidbit of information regarding sex. But not everything you hear is true.

Now, let's discuss some myths around sex that are pretty popular.

Myth #1: Everybody is doing it.

You might have heard this line from a friend or a movie character who casually dismisses the idea that sex should be considered carefully. Of course, this is a petty excuse, but many young people tend to believe this.

Your reason to have sex should never be because of hype. Choosing to be intimate with someone is a personal choice. Just because your friends are doing it and flaunting their sexual escapades does not mean you have to do it. And one more thing— just because you have done it before does not mean you have to make it a regular activity.

Myth #2: Pulling out can't make her pregnant.

As mentioned before, withdrawal is a less efficient birth control method.

The sperm is not only present during the ejaculation but even before it. The fluid that leaks during an erection, also called pre-cum, also bears sperms.

Remember that it only takes a single sperm to impregnate a girl. Not wearing condoms and using other contraception significantly increases your risk of pregnancy, even if you use withdrawal every time you have sex.

Myth #3: Girls cannot get pregnant if they have sex during their period.

Aside from the fact that this is unhygienic, having intercourse with a girl who is menstruating does not guarantee the impossibility of pregnancy. While pregnancy is highly unlikely to happen, the chance is still there.

The ovulation stage of their menstrual cycles is the period when women are most fertile. It happens about 12 to 16 days before the beginning of their next period. Meanwhile, some women have shorter cycles. It means that their ovulation stage starts early. So, unless you are very sure about the schedules of your body (or your partner's body), getting pregnant remains a possibility.

Myth #4: Real-life sex is merely like what you see in porn.

Porn may be an introduction to many teenagers. So, they think that the seemingly perfect bodies of the actresses, acrobatic performances, and quick orgasms are a "thing" in real life.

Porn actors are paid to make the video entertaining. What you see in porn is not a standard sex practice. Sex is imperfect in real life. You get thirsty, take breaks, act clumsily, and get awkward.

Myth #5: Birth control is the girl's responsibility.

Your decision to have sex is shared, so it is only fitting that you both take responsibility for using contraception. Guys should always use condoms as an extra barrier to prevent unplanned pregnancies and avoid the spread of STDs.

Myth #6: A girl does not get pregnant when having sex for the first time.

Having unprotected sex means a high chance of pregnancy, which also applies to having sex for the first time.

CHAPTER 7

WHAT HAPPENS ONLINE

W e are now living in the digital age where everything from personal to professional and recreational life happens at the tip of our fingertips with an electronic device. It is normal to see youths glued to their smartphones, playing, watching, or socializing. That being said, how younger people deal with their relationships nowadays dramatically differs from how the older generations did it during their time. These changes present us with room for learning— both for parents and children.

Teenagers can talk and meet with their love interests and take their relationship further through digital communication tools we currently find online. Pew Research Center reveals that about 35% of American teenagers (ages 13 to 17) have been romantically involved with another person they met online, and about 18% have remained in a romantic relationship. It further demonstrates that digital technology has radically shaped teens' behavior nowadays (Lenhart et al., 2020).

A lot of teenage interactions today occur online or through social media. From flirting to breaking up, social media and mobile phones are woven into teens' romantic lives. Online spaces play a major role in how teens flirt, woo, and communicate with potential and current flames. Social media is the top venue for flirting ranging from entry-level (friending them, sharing funny or interesting things) to more advanced (flirtatious messages, sexy or flirty picture or videos). It is also a place to publicly demonstrate their affection and show support for other's romantic relationships.

Despite the convenience the internet provides when it comes to communication and connection building, we cannot deny that this also opens up risks to not just your personal safety, but also your relation-ships with the people in your life, especially for youth.

Online Dating

Not all online romance are the same. Some in-volve online chats and phone calls only, while others include in-person meetings. The cyber world offers solace to teens who feel shy and awkward about en-gaging in face-to-face conversations with a potential love interest. As a shy teen, for example, may boldly approach new people in an online chat room. A teen with low self-esteem may find self-assurance when she's sitting behind a screen. For teenagers who strug-gle with anxiety, in particular, online dating may be the easiest and less stressful way of trying to make a connection. You can find like-mined peers and a com-munity on the internet that can help deal with the tur-bulence of adolescence.

However, for parents, dating may sound "too early" until their children are at least in their 30s. We can only imagine their horrified looks when their teenagers confess to online dating. However, the real-ity shows that many teenagers are hooked on socializ-ing online, including dating.

Many of our interactions happen online through messaging apps and social media. It is no longer surprising to learn if your friends have met their dates or finally succeeded in confessing their feelings to their crushes through these online spaces. This method is simply the norm to convey your interest and intentions directly or subtly.

To point it out, social media tops the list of venues for flirting with young people like you. If there is someone you are interested in, you can search for them on social media, befriend them, and start your friendship from there. It seems to be a more accessible and more brilliant move than approaching your love interest in real life. Many would agree that this strategy makes it more comfortable for both parties to gauge each other before heading to the next level of the relationship.

Below are several tips that you can apply in the high-risk field of online dating:

Never compromise your identity with anyone. It includes keeping your usernames, passwords, social security numbers, and banking information to yourself. Scammers can be creative, but one thing that you must never forget is to never share these crucial details, especially with people you just met online. You must never send money for any reason, even if they say it is an emergency or for your parents. Furthermore, it would be wise to keep the most precise details, such as your full names, addresses, birthdate, and personal information to yourself.

Limit your shared information on social media. You can tweak the filters and privacy settings in your Facebook, Twitter, Instagram, and other social media accounts for safety. Keep as little information as possible visible to strangers because the less they know, the better!

Do some background research to find out exactly who you're talking to. Unfortunately, catfishing is a thing; but fortunately, this can be deterred by doing video chats. If someone refuses to have a video chat with you every time, it is safe to say they are hiding something.

To get a feel for the person you are going to date:
- Reach out to your mutual friends.
- Ask whether the person is trustworthy or otherwise.

+ Feel free to utilize the reverse image search trick to double-check if the photo the other person has used is stolen.

Make sure to go on safe dates. There is power in numbers, so it helps to go on a double or group date first or until you can trust the person enough to go on a date alone. Always do dates during daylight hours and in public places. Do not invite them over to your home or go along with them to their own home. Be sure to inform your friends or family where you are going, and ensure that you prepare for an exit strategy should things go awry.

Be on the lookout for red flags. Learning to spot red flags can save your life. Here are some of them:

+ They have an unclear or incomplete profile.
+ They have no respect for digital boundaries.
+ They send sexually-explicit content and messages straightaway.
+ They get easily irked when you are late in replying.

Online Predators

We cannot dispute that social media has revolutionized our digital lifestyle. Nevertheless, it has two sides: benefits and downsides. Indeed, we can easily communicate and share everything about us and around us, but all of these can also expose us to certain risks, which includes online predators.

The primary concerns with teens dating online involve privacy and safety. Numerous adult predators lurk online in the guise of a seemingly harmless fellow teenager who "just wants to have a good time." These black-hearted individuals lure trusting teenagers into sexual relationships or steal their identities.

You need to be aware of this harsh reality and be cautious in approaching any online relationship. Be extra careful in using dating services that adults typically use.

Another cause of concern is the behind-the-screen behavior many of us develop. We tend to be bolder with our words and actions online than in person. We feel safe saying things that we would typically hesitate to say face-to-face with others. Consequently, we tend to share things that we would rather hide.

Sexting and Sending Sensitive Photos Online

Sexting means using your phone to send sexy message or naked photographs of yourself. The same thing goes with sharing sensitive information and private photos, even with your boyfriends or girlfriends. For example, sharing your Facebook password with your boyfriend or girlfriend because you consider it a sign of trust can be an issue after a breakup. You have to remember that there are certain things that you have to keep private, even from a romantic partner. And these include your social media passwords, risqué photos, and banking details.

Remember that whatever you post online will forever be there. Even when you have already deleted your post, you cannot be sure that someone hasn't taken a screenshot of it and will use it against you. If in the wrong hands, a sexting thread can perpetuate bullying, emotional abuse, revenge porn, harassment, embarrassment, low self-esteem, even depression. In some cases, teens can get into serious trouble for sexting because of laws about child pornography.

You may be tech-savvy, just like most young people nowadays, but it does not mean that you are tech safe. Although you can navigate apps with ease, you must also establish the resilience to deal with an issue by building and maintaining online relationships—and protecting yourself from online predators is one of them.

Cyberbullying

Bullying, in any form, is never okay. It has put many young lives through hell. Most often, bullying can lead to mental health issues such as anxiety, lower self-esteem, and depression. It may teach kids to skip classes, ultimately affecting their grades and school performance. The most severe consequence of bullying is that bullied teens are at a higher risk of self-harm and suicide than their peers.

Some teenagers tend to be more likely targets of bullies. These include the disabled, ethnic and religious minorities, and LGBTQ teens.

Now, when a teen uses a device and the internet to target, harass, embarrass, and threaten a fellow teenager, this is what we call cyberbullying. Cyberbullying can be any of the following:

- Pranking a person's smartphone
- Posting hurtful or embarrassing messages, images, and videos
- Sharing or posting someone's private messages, photos, and videos
- Sending malicious and mean texts or emails
- Making online threats
- Spreading malicious secrets or rumors online
- Being rude or mean to a person during an online game
- Hacking into a person's social networking or gaming account or profile

Cyberbullying is an alarming issue among young people like you today. It is growing rampant since bullies can harass their targets anonymously. And since bullies tend to act more aggressively under disguise, they can say or do anything online to destroy their target. Like physical bullying, cyberbullying has significant consequences:

- Emotional: anger, isolation, humiliation, and powerlessness
- Mental: anxiety, depression, low self-esteem, suicidal thoughts, self-harm, and academic issues

- Behavioral: skipping school, using alcohol and drugs, and bringing weapons to school
- Physical: eating disorders, sleep disturbances or insomnia, and gastrointestinal issues

If you experience cyberbullying, it is crucial to document and report the behavior. Here's what you should do:

- Do not respond to the messages and never forward them to others.
- Document cyberbullying instances. Save and print screenshots of postings, letters, emails, etc. You can also record the dates, times, and descriptions of when the cyberbullying happened. Use these pieces of evidence to report to the proper authorities.
- Block the cyberbully and edit the privacy settings of your social media profiles.
- Inform adults around you like your parents, guardians, or teachers that you are being bullied online.
- Report cyberbullying to your school, online service providers, and law enforcement.

Pornography

Decades ago, pornography was hard to access. You need to buy them in the form of VHS videos, CDs, and DVDs. But because of the internet era, even sexually curious kids can access it online.

Before, porn was limited to images and videos, but nowadays, you can play it in the form of online or mobile porn games.

Many teenagers who watch porn videos do it out of curiosity at first, but it has become their habit later on. A study shows that 62.1% of girls and 93.2% of boys out of 563 participants were exposed to online pornography during their adolescence (Sabina et al., 2008).

Sadly, regular exposure to porn causes negative impacts on young people, such as:

- Imitation of improper behaviors
- Early stimulation of sexual activities
- Unhealthy intervention with the normal sexual development process
- Development of negative attitude toward sex
- Development of harmful sexual behavior

♦ Emotional side effects include anxiety, guilt, shame, confusion, and nightmares

You must remember that the people you see in porn videos are actors whose bodies do not look like the average person's body. Many of them have gone through cosmetic procedures to enhance their features. Moreover, the sexual acts you see them perform do not reflect what people do in real life. Their expressions and actions are intentionally exaggerated to make the video more entertaining for the audience. In short, what you see in porn are unrealistic portrayals and do not reflect what couples usually do during intercourse.

Another negative representation of pornography is that people, especially women, are being objectified. The male actors treat females as mere sex dolls who obey their every desire without question. Pornography teaches you that sexual partners are merely consumable objects, not people who should be cherished and respected.

There is also an apparent lack of verbal or nonverbal communication between actors before, during, and after the sex acts. Porn actors often do not use condoms or other birth control methods, conveying the false message that "doing it raw" makes the sexual experience more pleasurable.

Understanding Porn Addiction

Porn addiction is becoming rampant among adults and young people alike. Everyone, especially the hormonally charged curious teen, can easily get hooked by immersing themselves in pornography.

As a teen, you have to realize that porn addiction can damage your mental, emotional, and sexual health. Teenagers regularly exposed to porn exhibit promiscuity, twisted views of love, impeded emotional intimacy in relationships, and depression. They also experience sexual dysfunctions and problems, such as sexually aggressive behaviors and erectile dysfunction.

When you see porn, your brain finds it hard to distinguish what is real or what is only an image, video, or game. It sets the attraction center of your brain into motion, generating irresistible feelings that kids your age find hard to manage. Typically, the brain's attraction center brings about feelings of happiness that help us fall in love. However, when porn triggers the attraction, teens psychologically experience what they see. As a result, they either desire to perform what they saw or get desensitized. Unfortunately, both can damage your ability to establish healthy and lifelong relationships.

Remember that you are at a crucial stage of development. Porn addiction can provide lasting damage to you. For such a reason, it is critical to seek help if you are addicted to porn. It would be best to find the right therapist with the right expertise.

Navigating sex and relationships as a teen will have its up and downs. As you experience it for yourself and encounter different situations, more questions will surely come up. In the next chapter, we will discuss some of the questions commonly asked by teens about sex and relationships.

CHAPTER 8

Q & A

As a teen, you have this urge to quench your thirst for answers because you want to catch up with countless changes that happen in and around you. Whether you believe it or not, this has been true to every adult since undergoing puberty, too. If you want to know something, spend time learning the answers to those questions running inside your head.

To help you, here is a roundup of the most popular questions about sex and relationships every teen is dying to know. (A little reminder, though—we may not cover everything you want to know, but consider this as a starting point to learn more specific topics to discuss with your parents, guardians, or any trustworthy adult in your life.)

Question #1: I have a crush on multiple people. Is that weird?

Do not worry because it is completely NORMAL. After all, crushes are all about admiring and liking somebody—and there are many amazing people out there! However, dating these crushes at the same time is another matter.

Simultaneously dating multiple people is not impossible. But then again, there are numerous things to consider if you want to try an open relationship. You must be truthful and honest to anyone you date. Discuss your rules of engagement, especially the details about how exclusive your dating will be. Remember that hiding these facts from the other person can create an enormous emotional disaster.

Question # 2: How will I know if I'm ready for sex?

You may feel pressured by your hormones and fellow teens, but you must understand that there is no need to rush. It is always advantageous to wait until you finally believe that you can handle the consequences and responsibilities connected with being intimate with your particular person.

Meanwhile, you may express your love through having long walks, intimate talks, holding hands, hugging, kissing, and enjoying your time together as kids.

Question #3: Is masturbation harmful to me? Is there such excessive masturbation?"

Masturbation helps you recognize what is pleasurable for you and what is not. It is an excellent method to help you feel connected with your body.

There are no definite rules on how often you should masturbate. As long as you do it privately, masturbating is harmless.

Question #4: Is first-time sex painful?

Usually, it is not. It also varies depending on the person. Some girls feel pain when their hymen gets stretched or tears, but others do not.

However, being too nervous or not ready for sex can hurt you. You can prevent physical pain during sexual intercourse by making sure that:

- Both of you are aroused or turned on
- Both of you are willing to have sex

+ Your genitals are well lubricated through genital fluids or artificial lubricant

For you to have a better sexual experience, you need to talk it over with your partner, especially, if the pain persists. It is also possible that you might have a more serious medical problem, so you should discuss this with a medical professional.

Finally, remember not to force yourself into having sex when you believe you are not ready to do it yet. Remember that sex is a big responsibility—far beyond wearing condoms, having birth control measures, or avoiding STD risks. You have every right to back down from it if you are not yet 100% ready.

Question #5: What do I do if sex hurts?

Some people feel pain whenever they have sex. They may feel itching or burning sensations for various reasons, such as:

+ Yeast infection or Urinary tract infection (UTI)
+ Allergy to latex condoms
+ Semen or sperm allergy

Better see your doctor if you experience pain whenever you have intercourse.

Q & A

Question #6: What if my partner wants to have sex, but I don't?

I can never emphasize this enough—nobody should force you to have sex with them. You should not have to engage in any sexual activity out of obligation or fear. Any form of forced sex is rape, regardless of whether the perpetrator is a stranger or your partner. A "no" means no, and both parties should understand this. Also, remember that drugs and alcohol can significantly impair judgment and diminish self-consciousness, increasing the probability of date rape. Hence, it would be wise to steer clear of situations that lead to this catastrophe.

However, if your partner continually pressures you or attempts to coerce you into having sex when you aren't ready, I think you should sincerely evaluate the relationship that you are in and whether it's the one for you.

Question #7: Is shaving or waxing your pubic hair okay even if you're a teen?

There is no rule against shaving when it comes to your own body, especially your pubes. There is no right or wrong. It is part of your body, so the ultimate decision is yours. Do whatever you are comfortable with.

Some people, including teens, trim, shave, or wax their pubic hair for hygienic reasons. If you are worried about what other people may think or say, then understand this: Being comfortable with your own body feels much better than following other people's opinions. Besides, there is no crime committed in shaving or trimming one's netherhairs!

Question #8: How can I get birth control without my parents finding it out?

Many teenagers find it hard to confess to their parents that they are already sexually active. Suppose you want to know your birth control options without discussing them with your parents. In that case, you can enlist the help of a healthcare professional like an adolescent medicine doctor, gynecologist, pediatrician, or any health provider.

The doctor-patient confidentiality lets you keep that you are already sexually active a secret since your doctor cannot tell your parent that you are taking contraceptives without your permission.

Q & A

Question #9: What is an orgasm? How should I know if I had one?

An orgasm is often described as an intense, wonderful physical feeling during masturbation or sex. The experience may differ from one person to another and can be different for the same person at separate times. For some, orgasms are subdued; for others, they are powerful.

During orgasm, you may feel your heart race and breathe quicker. You will also feel your pelvic muscles contract and immediately relax, followed by a wave of feeling that can be both emotional and pleasurable.

Question #10: I think I'm gay. What should I do about it?

Many teenagers get attracted to the same sex or the same and opposite sexes. It often leads to the notion that they may be homosexual or bisexual. You must understand that puberty is only the starting point of exploring sexual attraction. Because you are still young, your feelings may still change over time. But if they do not change at all, it is perfectly okay.

Regardless of what other people may see in you, you have to learn to love yourself. Other people may not be able to accept you for who you are, but it does not mean that you have to love yourself less. Being a gay, lesbian, bisexual, or transgender youth does not make you less of a beautiful person.

Question #11: How do I know if I'm asexual?

Have you ever had a crush? Have you ever considered someone sexy or hot?

An asexual person (also called "ace") does not experience or desire sexual attraction. You can kiss or have sex with anybody, but you are still identified as asexual. How? Asexuality is about attraction, not action. You can be somebody's boyfriend or girlfriend, kiss them, or have sex with them, but that doesn't mean you are sexually attracted. You can be asexual even if:

- You think someone is beautiful, handsome, or cute. Acknowledging someone's good looks does not automatically mean that you are attracted to them.

- You are dating because romantic attraction is different from sexual attraction. Many asexuals build relationships even if they are not so interested in sex.

- You masturbate. Masturbation can be done as a way to relieve stress.

- You have fallen in love. While sex is considered the ultimate expression of love, it cannot be equated to love itself. Some can be in love without thinking about sex.

- You have not done any of the things mentioned earlier. Some asexuals are not interested in romantic relationships, do not masturbate, or have sex.

Question #12: How do you know when the relationship is over? Are there any tell-tale signs?

Relationships always involve emotions and feelings. These factors can make a relationship beautiful and complex.

However, something is amiss if your relationship brings negative emotions and feelings. Talk about it with your partner—the sooner, the better. If your issues are not solved even after trying to fix them, it is time to move on.

Question #13: Is it necessary to "love" a person first before committing to a relationship?

Liking or loving someone is a great starting point for a committed relationship. Nevertheless, both parties should always take time to improve their skills to maintain trust and respect within the relationship.

If you want to date with marriage in mind, you should consider good matching (such as similar cultural, religious, and financial values).

Question #14: How long should my partner and I hold an issue?

Here's the truth: Holding on to anger and pain will hurt you and rob you of energy and love. The good rule of thumb is to strive to solve your issues within 24 hours. Talk about what bothers you immediately because procrastination will only push the unresolved matters behind you.

Everybody makes mistakes; what is essential is that we learn from them. When couples try to discuss their mistakes respectfully and learn from them, their relationship will steadily improve.

Question #15: What is the worst thing about being in a relationship?

That is being in a TOXIC relationship— the type that continuously generates distrust, anger, insecurity, anxiety, and negative emotions. It is by far, much better to remain single than to involve yourself in a toxic relationship.

A teenage romantic relationship should inspire you, not pull you into the depths of despair.

Question #16: My boyfriend (or girlfriend) cheated on me. Is our relationship worth saving?

It depends on the situation. Some relationships are best ended with the first issue of infidelity. Some are worth saving, especially when you can see that the other person is genuinely sorry and that you find in your heart that you can forgive their two-timing.

Still, some people should learn from their mistakes. Breaking up with them offers an excellent opportunity to reevaluate their actions. If you believe that your relationship is already unhealthy, it is best to end it.

Questions #17: I'm a virgin and curious if it is true that sex is fun and feels good.

Yes, sex can be fun and feel good, but not all time. It is hard to separate the act of sex from a person you are doing it with or the person you are. If you are not ready to have sex or you are doing it in the wrong relationship, or with the wrong person, you will likely not enjoy it. But if you feel comfortable and care about sex and truly feel ready for it, then yes. It can be painful or awkward the first time, which is totally normal. There is a lot of pressure, and it will take few times to figure out what you and your partner enjoy.

Questions #18: My partner wants to have sex. How do I know if my partner is just using me?

If in a relationship where one person is ready to have sex but the other isn't, it can be stressful because you don't want to compromise when you feel unprepared. If your partner tries to pressure you into having sex, they aren't thinking about what matters most to you. Anyone who pressure others into having sex only looks to satisfy their feelings and yearnings. If you are having sex because you are afraid of losing partner, then it may be a sign that you are not in the right relationship. Your partner should make you feel appreciated, respected, and supported, not pressure or make you feel uncomfortable. If they care about you, they won't force to do something you are not ready for. Thus talk with your partner about how you feel. If they are the right person, they will understand.

Questions #19: Is it suitable to bring up past situations in my current relationship or should I focus on the current issue?

Start with the current issue. Bring up the past if they shed light on the current one. Most importantly, though, when you raise issues, your job is to focus on your part of what went wrong. Let your partner explore their part. Otherwise, you risk getting into criticism and blame, neither of which have high odds of leading to learning and change.

CONCLUSION

Now that you know many things about sex education, I expect you to become a responsible citizen even at a young age. This sex education book will not only protect you through your teenage years but will also mold and prepare you to become a good adult.

Your teen years are your battleground. At this stage, you are trained to respond appropriately to challenges in your surroundings and life in general. At this stage, it is vital to maintain a good relationship with your parents or any trusted adult who can provide you with additional knowledge and protection before you can be completely ready to face adult life.

Bear in mind that your parents are always there to support and guide you. Unless there is something wrong with your parents, maintaining open communication with them should be your priority. There's no reason that you hide anything from them. For one, they have been through these things, and because you are their child, they can fully protect you from bad individuals if they know what is happening to you 24/7.

Just because they have to maintain their authority does not mean that they can't understand your point of view. Remember that your parents were once teens like you, and they could have done worse during their youth. But regardless of what they have been through, surely they want to spare you going through bad experiences.

There is nothing wrong with discussing sex education with your parents. Sometimes you may feel awkward and embarrassed to discuss things like this because our society led us to believe that sex is something dirty. This is not valid. Sex education can even bond a daughter to her mother and a son to his father. Communication gaps exist because teens quickly adapt to their peers, readily believing what other teens tell them. But remember that families are different.

Your friends may come from a dysfunctional family with different values, so they think it's safer to hide things from their parents. But with you, who grew up with your parents' love, care, and protection, there's no reason to hide anything from them, especially things about sex. Sometimes, they are just overprotective because they don't want you to do something you will regret later.

Heard that "Dad or Mom knows best?" Of course, they do!

So before you choose the wrong path towards adulthood, seek your parents' advice. Do not feel embarrassed or awkward asking them about things that trigger your curiosity. It is normal for teens to be curious about sex, and parents know this. And they are happy to see that you trust them enough to discuss these things with them rather than discover them in other people's company. Remember that parents are given to you to guide you through your journey in life. Trust them and be grateful when they are there for you.

With the knowledge you have found in this book, you can make better and informed decisions about what you want for yourself and your future. Be empowered to take control of your body and make the right decision in your relationships.

If you found this book useful, help other teens like you who may also need the information and advice from this book by leaving a review. I would be incredibly thankful.

REFERENCES

Act Youth. (n.d.). *Romantic Relationships in Adolescence*. Sexual Development - ACT for Youth. https://actforyouth.net/sexual_health/romantic.cfm

Action Canada for Sexual Health and Rights. (2019, July 23). What Young People Want and Need for their Sex-Ed | Action Canada for Sexual Health and Rights. https://www.actioncanadashr.org/resources/sexual-health-info/sex-ed/what-young-people-want-and-need-their-sex-ed

American Psychological Association. (2017, March). Five Sex Facts That Will Shock You. https://www.apa.org/pi/aids/youth/sex-facts

Canadian Paediatric Society. (2018, March). Your teen's sexual orientation. https://caringfork-ids.cps.ca/handouts/preteens-and-teens/teens_sexual_orientation

Center for Disease and Control Prevention. (2021, November 15). *About Teen Pregnancy | CDC*. https://www.cdc.gov/teenpreg-nancy/about/index.htm

Center for Disease Control and Prevention. (2018, June 22). Over Half of U.S. Teens Have Had Sexual Intercourse by Age 18, New Report Shows. CDC- National Center for Health Statistics. https://www.cdc.gov/nchs/press-room/nchs_press_re-leases/2017/201706_NSFG.htm

Center for Disease Control and Prevention. (2021, April). Adolescents and Young Adults | Pre-vention | STDs | CDC. https://www.cdc.gov/std/life-stages-popula-tions/adolescents-youngadults.htm

Cleveland Clinic. (2019, April 12). Birth Control Options & Types: Risks & Effectiveness. Cleveland Clinic. https://my.cleve-landclinic.org/health/articles/11427-birth-control-options#:%7E:text=natural%20fam-ily%20planning.-

,How%20effec-
tive%20is%20it%3F,can%20be%2090%20per-
cent%20effective

Cleveland Clinic. (2022). Genital Warts: HPV, STD,
Symptoms, Causes, Treatment.
https://my.clevelandclinic.org/health/dis-
eases/4209-genital-warts#:%7E:text=Geni-
tal%20warts%20are%20a%20type,Some%20
warts%20are%20very%20small

Discover U.S. government information. U.S. Government Publishing Office. (2003, January 16).
Retrieved June 12, 2022, from
https://www.govinfo.gov/

Detailed STD Facts - Gonorrhea. (2022, April 12).
Center for Disease Control and Prevention.
https://www.cdc.gov/std/gonor-
rhea/stdfact-gonorrhea-detailed.htm

Guttmacher Institute. (2016, September 9). Fewer
U.S. Teens Are Receiving Formal Sex Education Now Than in the Past.
https://www.guttmacher.org/news-re-
lease/2016/fewer-us-teens-are-receiving-for-
mal-sex-education-now-past

Health Behavior News Service. (2008, March 13).
Comprehensive Sex Education Might Re-
duce Teen Pregnancies. Newswise.

https://www.newswise.com/articles/com-prehensive-sex-education-might-reduce-teen-pregnancies

Hepatitis B | CDC. (2021, October 12). Centers for Disease Control and Prevention. https://www.cdc.gov/hepatitis/hbv/index.htm

Holland, N. (2017, October 27). *Teens prefer hasty hookups over dedicated dating.* The Observer. Retrieved June 12, 2022, from https://www.thechurchillobserver.com/features/2017/10/25/teens-prefer-hasty-hookups-dedicated-dating/

How Effective Are Cervical Caps? | Cervical Cap Effectiveness. (n.d.). Planned Parenthood. https://www.plannedparenthood.org/learn/birth-control/cervical-cap/how-effective-are-cervical-caps#:%7E:text=The%20cervical%20cap%20is%20a,get%20pregnant%20within%20a%20year

Kansky, J., & Allen, J. P. (2018). Long-Term Risks and Possible Benefits Associated with Late Adolescent Romantic Relationship Quality. Journal of Youth and Adolescence, 47(7), 1531–1544. https://doi.org/10.1007/s10964-018-0813-x

References

Langmaid, S. (2016, June 21). Pull Out Method (Withdrawal). WebMD. https://www.webmd.com/sex/birth-control/pull-out-withdrawal#:%7E:text=Pulling%20out%20isn't%20a,5%20%2D%2D%20would%20get%20pregnant

Lenhart, A., Anderson, M., & Smith, A. (2020, May 30). *Teens, technology and romantic relationships*. Pew Research Center: Internet, Science & Tech. Retrieved June 12, 2022, from https://www.pewresearch.org/internet/2015/10/01/teens-technology-and-romantic-relationships/#:~:text=Overall%2C%2035%25%20of%20American%20teens,currently%20in%20a%20romantic%20relationship

Manning, W., Longmore, M., & Giordano, P. (2005, June). Adolescents' Involvement in Non-Romantic Activity. ScienceDirect. Retrieved April 21, 2022, from https://www.sciencedirect.com/science/article/abs/pii/S0049089X04000377?via%3Dihub

Mayo Clinic. (2022, May 17). *Trichomoniasis - Symptoms and causes*. https://www.mayoclinic.org/diseases-conditions/trichomoniasis/symptoms-causes/syc-

20378609#:%7E:text=Trichomonia-
sis%20is%20caused%20by%20a,%2C%20wo
men%2C%20and%20sometimes%20men

MyHealthAlberta, & Healthwise Staff. (2021, June
16). Barrier Methods of Birth Control: Care
Instructions. Myhealth.Alberta.Ca.
https://myhealth.alberta.ca/Health/after-
careinformation/pages/condi-
tions.aspx?hwid=uf9648#:~:text=Spermi-
cide%20used%20alone%20does%20not,sper-
micide%20without%20a%20doctor's%20pre-
scription

Osterman, M., Hamilton, B., Martin, J., Driscoll, A.,
& Valenzuela, C. (2021). Births: Final Data
for 2020. Births: Final Data for 2020.
https://doi.org/10.15620/cdc:112078

Petanjek, Z., Judaš, M., ŠImić, G., Rašin, M. R.,
Uylings, H. B. M., Rakic, P., & Kostović,.
(2011). Extraordinary neoteny of synaptic
spines in the human prefrontal cortex. Pro-
ceedings of the National Academy of Sci-
ences, 108(32), 13281–13286.
https://doi.org/10.1073/pnas.1105108108

Raising Children Network (Australia) Limited.
(n.d.). Relationships and romance: pre-teens
and teenagers. Raising Children Network.
https://raisingchildren.net.au/pre-

teens/communicating-relationships/roman-
tic-relationships/teen-relationships

Relationships and romance: pre-teens and teenagers.
(2021, September 14). Raising Children Network. https://raisingchildren.net.au/pre-
teens/communicating-relationships/roman-
tic-relationships/teen-relation-
ships#:%7E:text=If%20your%20child%20is%
20in,sexual%20behav-
iour%20at%20some%20stage

Reproductive Health Teen Pregnancy. (2021, No-
vember 15). Center for Disease Control and
Prevention. https://www.cdc.gov/teenpreg-
nancy/about/index.htm#:~:text=Preg-
nancy%20and%20birth%20are%20signifi-
cant,adolescence%20gradu-
ate%20from%20high%20school

Rohatgi, A. (2015, February 23). Understanding the
psychology behind teenage attraction. The
Companion. https://thecompanion.in/un-
derstanding-the-psychology-behind-teenage-
attraction#:%7E:text=Accord-
ing%20to%20various%20re-
searches%2C%20there,of%20lik-
ing%20and%20physical%20attractiveness

Sabina, C., Wolak, J., & Finkelhor, D. (2008). The
Nature and Dynamics of Internet

Pornography Exposure for Youth Under 18. University of New Hampshire. https://www.unh.edu/ccrc/resource/nature-dynamics-internet-pornography-exposure-youth-under-18

Sexuality: pre-teens and teenagers. (2021, April 27). Raising Children Network. https://raisingchildren.net.au/pre-teens/development/puberty-sexual-development/teenage-sexuality

Shipman, Matt, and Sarah Wild says: "*Study Highlights Fluid Sexual Orientation in Many Teens.*" NC State News, 4 Nov. 2019, https://news.ncsu.edu/2019/11/teen-sexual-orientation/

Stanford Children's Health. (n.d.). default - Stanford Children's Health. https://www.stanfordchildrens.org/en/topic/default?id=sexually-transmitted-diseases-in-adolescents-90-P01654

The Nemours Foundation. (2022, January). Chlamydia (for teens) - primary children's hospital. KidsHealth. Retrieved June 6, 2022, from https://kidshealth.org/PrimaryChildrens/en/teens/std-chlamydia.html

References

The Nemours Foundation. (2018, May). The Diaphragm (for teens) - primary children's hospital. KidsHealth. Retrieved June 6, 2022, from https://kidshealth.org/PrimaryChildrens/en/teens/contraception-diaphragm.html?ref=search

The Nemours Foundation. (2022, January). Genital herpes (for teens) - primary children's hospital. KidsHealth. Retrieved June 6, 2022, from https://kidshealth.org/PrimaryChildrens/en/teens/std-herpes.html

The Nemours Foundation. (2022, January). HIV and AIDS (for teens) - primary children's hospital. KidsHealth. Retrieved June 6, 2022, from https://kidshealth.org/PrimaryChildrens/en/teens/std-hiv.html

The Nemours Foundation. (2021, January). Pelvic Inflammatory Disease (PID) (for teens) - primary children's hospital. KidsHealth. Retrieved June 6, 2022, from https://kidshealth.org/PrimaryChildrens/en/teens/std-pid.html

The Nemours Foundation. (2022, January). Public Lice (Crabs) (for teens) - primary children's hospital. KidsHealth. Retrieved June 6, 2022, from https://kidshealth.org/PrimaryChildrens/en/teens/std-lice.html

The Nemours Foundation. (2018, October). Syphilis (for teens) - primary children's hospital. KidsHealth. Retrieved June 6, 2022, from https://kidshealth.org/PrimaryChildrens/en/teens/std-syphilis.html

The Nemours Foundation. (2022, January). The IUD (for teens)-primary children's hospital. KidsHealth. Retrieved June 6, 2022, from https://kidshealth.org/PrimaryChildrens/en/teens/contraception-iud.html?WT.ac=t-ra

The Nemours Foundation. (2022, January). Birth control pill (for teens) - primary children's hospital. KidsHealth. Retrieved June 6, 2022, from https://kidshealth.org/PrimaryChildrens/en/teens/contraception-birth.html?WT.ac=t-ra

The Nemours Foundation. (2022, January). Emergency contraception (for teens) - primary children's hospital. KidsHealth. Retrieved June 6, 2022, from https://kidshealth.org/PrimaryChildrens/en/teens/contracetption-emergency.html?WT.ac=t-ra

The Nemours Foundation. (2022, January). Birth control methods: How well do they work? (for teens) - primary children's hospital.

References

KidsHealth. Retrieved June 6, 2022, https://kidshealth.org/PrimaryChildrens/en/teens/bc-chart.html?WT.ac=t-ra

The British Psychological Society. (2016, July). Teenagers in love | The Psychologist. The Psychologist. Retrieved March 6, 2022, from https://thepsychologist.bps.org.uk/volume-29/july/teenagers-love

Why is teenage pregnancy on the rise? – Terasolartisans.com. (n.d.). Terasolartisans.Com. https://www.terasolartisans.com/john/notes-of-a-writers/why-is-teenage-pregnancy-on-the-rise/

World Health Organization. (n.d.). *Adolescent pregnancy*. World Health Organization. Retrieved June 12, 2022, from https://www.who.int/news-room/factsheets/detail/adolescent-pregnancy